Simple. Clear. Mc
Royal Hamel's bo
neighbours for C
we can overcome our fears and, with confidence, make
evangelism "mission possible" for the most timid amongst
us. A great read!

David Arrol Macfarlane
Billy Graham Evangelistic Association of Canada

A very worthwhile, encouraging and easy-to-read book with
so many practical suggestions for witnessing that we are left
without excuse!

Jean Shannon
Missionary to Argentina with her husband,
Jack, for almost forty years

I believe when we come to a conversation about the spread
of the gospel it can often be more like untangling a pair
of earphones, leaving many frustrated, confused, and afraid.
Royal Hamel has untangled the earphones for us and allows
us to listen to a very practical, simple, and natural expression
of evangelism. Instead of leaving it to the professionals or
the gifted, speaking of Jesus is now for the everyday believer
no matter his or her personality type. If you are frustrated
or have a great desire to share your faith but do not know
where to begin, *Unmuzzle Your Inner Sheep* will be an
encouragement to you.

Pastor David Robinson
Grace Bible Church

In *Unmuzzle Your Inner Sheep,* Pastor Royal Hamel pastorally and firmly dispels excuses and misconceptions about evangelism and brings it back to what it was meant to be, Christ-followers bearing witness to Jesus. Royal's stories are a great reminder about how easy telling others about Jesus really is, and his passion shines as he inspires all believers to engage in this great joy of planting the seeds of the gospel in the lives of the people we encounter every day. A great read and a valuable resource!

Pete Burrill
Pastor of Emmanuel Reformed Church

As a self-confessing Evangelical, I am by definition committed to being a witness to who Christ is and what he has done for sinners, myself included. But ah, how often I fail to be what I declare myself to be. This new book by Royal Hamel is a great tonic—but not only for me, but for any who regard themselves as committed followers of Christ but find sharing their faith difficult. May we take Hamel's advice to heart and seek every avenue we can to give a reason for the hope that we have—and God may own our words for his glory!

Michael A. G. Haykin
Professor of Church History, The Southern Baptist
Theological Seminary

My first thought when I began reading Royal Hamel's new book, *Unmuzzle Your Inner Sheep,* was that either I would be bored, "I've heard this all before," or I would feel guilty, "I am not doing enough to reach lost people." To my surprise I felt neither of those responses. Rather I was invited into a conversation that was both honest and natural. In fact, if I could summarize the book in a phrase it would be "Witnessing, as natural as breathing." Royal does an amazing job of leading his readers to see that for a believer, sharing Jesus is to be woven into the natural fabric of our everyday lives. To simply keep our hearts ready and our eyes open for the myriad of opportunities that God brings our way to simply share a "word" that opens the opportunity for Jesus to be engaged. The stories Royal uses are inspiring, the quotes powerful, and when I finished the book I was invigorated to "unmuzzle my inner sheep." I highly recommend this book.

Rev. David Hearn
President of the Christian and
Missionary Alliance in Canada

I have known Royal for thirty years, and his book is a poignant illustration of the life he lives. He explains and illustrates how he refers to Christ in everyday conversations, that it is truly "easier than most of us have been led to believe." You will find great benefit in reading, interacting over, and applying what you learn here.

Jim Klaas
Discipleship consultant,
Networkchurch.ca

Followers of Jesus possess Good News that must be shared! And it is up to *yo*u! No more passing the buck to pastors or evangelists! In this book, Royal encourages and challenges you through stories that will not only inspire but also remove all the excuses as to why you don't share the gospel. If you want to stay safe and silent, do not read this book. But if you know that you need to learn how to share the Good News that has changed your life, this book is for you!

Pastor Kellen Wiersma
Crossings Alliance Church

Royal Hamel comes well qualified, with over two decades of church ministry in North and South America, to address a "forgotten essential" of the church. *Witnessing* is an old term, straight from the New Testament. Interestingly, our judicial system continues to depend heavily on "witnesses." But the church of today is stumbling along without them. The author also links "witnessing" with "repentance." This book is a *must read* for our day.

Dr. Arnold Cook
Former President of the C&MA Canada

One of the most profound struggles for most Christians focuses on how we should share our faith with others. Do we let our actions speak for themselves? Do we proclaim Christ on the street corners or on the factory floor? Royal Hamel has the uncanny ability to engage his audience in a practical conversation about witnessing and evangelism. *Unmuzzle Your Inner Sheep* reads like a conversation one would have with Royal in a local coffee shop: practical, readable, biblical, Spirit-filled. The questions at the end of each chapter serve as an excellent outline for any small group discussion or personal reflection. A church's approach to evangelism needs to begin with this book.

Keith Knight
Executive Director of the Canadian
Christian Business Federation

From the first page to the last, Royal Hamel shouts the clear call of Scripture, all who follow Jesus must testify to the Good News. *Unmuzzle Your Inner Sheep* challenges us with the privilege and the responsibility to be witnesses in word and action to the life found in Jesus Christ alone. Thankfully Royal does not leave you with just a challenge. Instead he helps you to start taking your own unique steps in a life journey of evangelism. *Unmuzzle Your Inner Sheep* is a must read for the timid, the shy, and the reluctant disciple of Jesus Christ.

Pastor Richard Stanley
Crossings Community Church

This is a wonderful book! For many Christians, the term "evangelism" has become a scary one. This book helps to address false foundational beliefs that lead to such fear as well as giving positive steps for developing a healthy understanding and practice of evangelism. Royal brings home the importance and ease of sharing our faith in a constructive, Spirit-filled way. I will be sure to have at least two copies in my own library, one for myself and one to loan out. I will also ensure that my church library has a copy and will be recommending it frequently!

Rev. David Williams
Priory Park Baptist Church

Royal Hamel has sounded a trumpet blast to the whole body of Christ. This book is a piercing clarion call, rousing believers to take up their God-given responsibility to share the gospel. Hamel spells out the under-lying reasons for our lack of witness and gives practical, compelling insights into how Christ-followers can successfully engage their world with the good news of Jesus Christ. This book is a "must read" for every Christian.

Ken Miles, Senior Pastor, Kitchener-Waterloo Christian Fellowship, President of Anchor Ministerial Fellowship, anchorministerial.org

In a comprehensive yet liberating fashion, Royal Hamel confronts our fears, misconceptions, and excuses and gently dismantles them. *Unmuzzle Your Inner Sheep* opens up biblical truth and is illustrated with numerous real-life examples. It is a must-read for believers desiring to become disciples! This book is carefully designed to engage both the casual reader as well as the serious Bible student. As a senior pastor, reading through Royal's book made me realize I had found an excellent small group resource to help equip our church pursue our vision of "developing fully devoted followers of Jesus." Without a doubt, this book will be a valuable addition to any leader's discipleship tool kit!

Jim Gordon,
Senior Pastor,
Elora Road Christian Fellowship

Royal Hamel calls attention to a vital component in the church which has for too long been neglected and ignored, namely, the call to evangelism. Hamel reminds the reader that evangelism is the task of every person who names the name of Christ and claims to be his follower. The present state of the church in our day is one of extreme apathy and inactivity. Hamel challenges the Christian reader in light of this reality, to rediscover the area of evangelism afresh from a firm biblical foundation. I would recommend this book to anyone who has a passion to share Christ.

Tony Costa, PhD
Professor, Toronto Baptist Seminary

Royal Hamel has written a realistic and truly motivating guide for anyone who wishes to share the good news of Jesus Christ with the everyday people in his or her life. So much of what he sets forth is "battle tested" and flows out of his daily personal practices. As a pastor, I plan to use this book as I train people in my congregation to share their faith with others.

John Fairchild,
Pastor of Congregational Care, Grace Community Church

Inspiring! That's how I describe Unmuzzle Your Inner Sheep. I rejoice that my friend Royal has decided to write this book. His stories always motivate me towards witness, since they are just ordinary everyday encounters from an intentional disciple maker. I know Royal as a man on mission. This is why he and his wife, Linda, equip the church through Talk the Walk workshops, designed to inspire even the most introverted person to be missional. We greatly benefited as a church, when we hosted their workshop for our people. What Royal shares with us works! He offers every believer the theology and praxis for an exciting life lived to the glory of our King Jesus.

Pastor Mike Stanley
Freedom House Church and Healing Centre Inc.

UNMUZZLE
Your Inner SHEEP

Liberating Believers to Share Jesus

Royal M. Hamel
Foreword by Dr. T.V. Thomas

Unless otherwise indicated, all Scripture quotations are taken from The Holy Bible, New International Version®, NIV® Copyright © 1973, 1978, 1984, 2011 by Biblica, Inc.™ Used by permission. • Scripture quotations marked (NASB) are taken from the NEW AMERICAN STANDARD BIBLE®, Copyright © 1960, 1962, 1963, 1968, 1971, 1972, 1973, 1975, 1977, 1995 by The Lockman Foundation. Used by permission. • Scripture quotations marked (NKJV) or "New King James Version" are taken from the New King James Version / Thomas Nelson Publishers, Nashville: Thomas Nelson Publishers, Copyright ©1982. Used by permission. All rights reserved. • The Holy Bible, English Standard Version (ESV) is adapted from the Revised Standard Version of the Bible, copyright Division of Christian Education of the National Council of the Churches of Christ in the U.S.A. All rights reserved.

Printed in Canada

ISBN: 978-1-77069-784-3

Word Alive Press
131 Cordite Road, Winnipeg, MB R3W 1S1
www.wordalivepress.ca

Library and Archives Canada Cataloguing in Publication

Hamel, Royal M., 1948-
      Unmuzzle your inner sheep : liberating believers to share Jesus / Royal M. Hamel.

ISBN 978-1-77069-784-3

      1. Witness bearing (Christianity). I. Title.

BV4520.H34 2013   248'.5   C2013-900849-7

Special discounts are available on quantity purchases by churches, church associations, educational institutions, and others.
For details, contact the author at:
Light the Darkness Ministries, 17A-218 Silvercreek Pkwy N
Suite 319, Guelph, ON, N1H 8E8
or at www.royalhamel.com.

To the memory of Professor Murray W. Downey, who first
inculcated in me a love for sharing the truth of Jesus,
and
To the memory of Mrs. Kay Roberts, mother of my wife,
Linda, who, though shy and reserved in temperament,
did what she could—she ardently pursued
and loved people into the kingdom

Table of Contents

Acknowledgments

Writing is largely a solitary task. However, anyone who has ever written has surely concluded that many people behind the scenes contributed to the publishing of their book. That is certainly the case with the book you hold in your hands.

I first of all acknowledge the generous support and encouragement of Frank and Karen McKellar, who were among the original believers in this idea and enabled me to begin this work.

I thank the various people who read the manuscript and offered many helpful suggestions. They include Ray Wiseman, David Wrathall, Pastor David Williams, Rev. Dr. Bob Penhearow, Peter and Sandra Hillen, Hugh Manary, Frances Wassink, Gordon Truscott, and last, but by no means least, my wife, Linda. Special thanks as well are due to my son, Jonathan, for his help at various times in guiding me through the complexities of Microsoft Word. A special word of acknowledgment is due to my three editors. The superb work of Lori Mackay, Krysia Lear, and Karen McKellar has been of immense value in the completion of this book.

I especially thank Rev. Dr. T. V. Thomas, director of the Centre for Evangelism and World Mission, for inspiring me years ago with his weekend Evangelism Alive Seminar. Some of my ideas on lifestyle evangelism were inspired by his excellent presentations.

I also thank noteworthy contributors like Rev. Dr. Bob Penhearow, Frances Wassink, Henry DeHaan, and David Wrathall, members of the board of Light the Darkness Ministries. They gave steady support and encouragement, especially when progress was slow and uneven. They never lost sight of the importance of the project and cheerfully prodded me to keep going. Thank you my friends.

Finally, I express my deepest appreciation and thanks to my wife, Linda, with whom I have been delighted to share thirty-eight years of marriage. She is my friend, the love of my life, the mother of our children and my mentor in the world of writing. She has been, and continues to be, my helpmate par excellence.

Foreword

History provides compelling evidence of the decline in evangelism when it is not intentionally emphasized and embraced as the primary task of the Christian and the Church. There is mounting evidence today in the Western Church that reaching spiritually lost people does not enjoy that top priority.

Royal Hamel's book is a bold invitation to make evangelism a priority again by encouraging, equipping, and empowering every believer to share Jesus with the unsaved in his or her circles of influence. For any congregation to be biblically missional its members need to be witnessing. Some approaches, methods, and strategies in evangelism may become irrelevant and ineffective with the change of times and cultures. However, personal witnessing remains universally relevant and effective. It can involve every follower of Christ, and the scope of impact is limitless. Ongoing personal witnessing is foundational for the sustainability and effectiveness of most other approaches in evangelism.

Hamel's motivation is close to God's heart—winning the lost. That was Christ's clear goal: *"For the Son of Man has come to seek and to save that which was lost"* (Luke 19:10 NKJV). Christ's teaching mandated that for the Church, and his ministry modeled that for his disciples. In Matthew 28:19, Jesus declared "Go...and make disciples of all nations" and in Acts 1:8, "You shall be My witnesses" (NASB).

The author passionately invites us to change our thinking about how we as Christians relate to unbelievers. Most of us live and work alongside many unbelievers for extended periods of time. As believers we are to intentionally discover ways to relate to unbelievers, spend time with them, and sow the seeds of the gospel. He encourages such ongoing engagement by defusing the common fears, fallacies, myths, and misconceptions Christians often have. Spiritual power can be released in our lives for effective witness, through prayer and the enabling of the Holy Spirit.

Royal exposes the fundamental reason why most followers of Christ do not witness. The root of the matter is their relationship with the Lord. The secret of being an everyday witness for Jesus flows out of our personal intimacy with Christ. Effective communication about Christ results from close communion with Christ. If he were truly the wellspring of our life, we would eagerly, earnestly, and enthusiastically talk about him. I am convinced there are more unbelievers ready to hear the Good News than there are believers to share it with them.

I trust that the following passages, which have encouraged me to persevere in my witnessing with all its inadequacies, will help you to share Jesus led by the Spirit:

Those who sow in tears shall reap with shouts of joy! He who goes out weeping, bearing the seed for sowing, shall come home with shouts of joy, bringing his sheaves with him (Psalm 126:5–6 ESV).

The fruit of the righteous is a tree of life, and whoever captures souls is wise (Proverbs 11:30 ESV).

And those who are wise shall shine like the brightness of the sky above; and those who turn many to righteousness, like the stars forever and ever" (Daniel 12:3 ESV).

Dr. T. V. Thomas
Director, Centre for Evangelism and World Mission
Regina, Canada

Introduction

Not that long ago I found myself eating lunch with a young Christian whom I shall call Maria. She was visiting our church and after the service that morning had decided to stay for lunch with the congregation. I quickly perceived that Maria was a passionate, intelligent young Christian with strong ideas.

One of Maria's pet peeves was witnessing. She said, "I don't agree that we Christians are called to share our beliefs. It's enough that we live out our faith in front of people." She was, in fact, annoyed by pastors and others who encouraged believers to witness verbally.

Because I knew what Scripture teaches on evangelism I was able to gently challenge her views and give her satisfactory answers. Maria and I parted on good terms, and I expressed the hope we would see each other again soon.

This exchange left me wondering how many other Christians believe that simply living out our faith before people serves as our primary way of witnessing. I have pastored a number of churches in Canada and have had the opportunity to serve as a missionary in Mexico and Argentina. Sadly, in all three countries, I have observed that the default way to witness for most Christians is to merely live out their faith rather than speaking about it.

Let us be clear that to live out our beliefs is certainly a part of witnessing. It is, in fact, very necessary, and the catchy little phrase "We need to walk the talk" sums it up very nicely. However, by itself, this saying teaches a half-truth, for Jesus clearly intended that we who possess the Good News should be speakers as well as doers. He uses our words as the means by which others come to believe in him.

I think the vast majority of us really want to honour Christ's command to follow him in full obedience. In fact, the title of this book, *Unmuzzle Your Inner Sheep,* explicitly accepts the premise that we Christ-followers are the sheep and he, Jesus, is the Shepherd who leads us.

I know there are multiplied thousands of sheepish sheep who long to be unmuzzled from crippling fears and ignorance so they can witness about the Jesus they follow. Indeed, the purpose of this book, as the sub-title suggests, is to empower believers in Jesus to share the Good News openly and transparently.

We know that the New Testament, from beginning to end, calls us to witness to the Christ who rescued us from darkness. The problem for most of us is simply that we have no idea where to begin.

This book is not primarily a "how to" manual that focuses on methods and techniques for evangelism. Rather, it zeroes in on the need to adopt a new way of thinking about how we relate to unbelievers. For example, many of us Christians for far too long have been content to hang around with people who believe and act just like we do. What if we decided to spend significant portions of our time in the presence of those who do not believe?

I know this sounds so simple that it comes close to insulting your intelligence. But trust me, it is a revolutionary idea that actually bears fruit. I have tried it. I am carrying this out on a regular basis. Here is what I have discovered: If you spend enough time with those who are outside the faith, sooner or later you will have opportunities to speak to them of the faith.

I congratulate each one of you who has picked up this book. Though we have not met personally, I think I may know a little bit about you. Are you one of those people who is passionate about sharing your faith? The mere fact you are perusing this particular book tells me you have a specialized interest. I would guess you are probably one of those people who is always looking and praying for opportunities to speak some word about Christ. You may even be one of those relatively rare people who already witnesses—but yearn to do it more effectively.

You may not fit this description at all. In fact, you may feel extremely tentative about all forms of witnessing. If totally candid, you might even admit to serious doubts you could ever be a witness for Christ. If so, you need to know that this book is very much for you as well. I promise you it is not about finding a newer and better method. It is not about prodding you to share with the person sitting next to you on the airplane. This entire book describes a new way of living.

And no, it's not a book just for the apostle Paul type of personality. You have probably met some of those happy-go-lucky extroverts who find witnessing as easy as cracking a smile. But what about people of a shyer bent? God made the shy and introverted temperament just as much as he made the bubbling, gregarious extrovert. Both types are of equal value before God, and both are of equal value in giving witness to Christ. However, introverts and extroverts are in no way obliged to share their witness in the same way. In chapter 9, I focus on how the introverted as well as the extroverted can become the witness Christ intended.

Witnessing is far easier than most of us have been led to believe. I simply cannot emphasize this enough. You may be tentative and uncertain about witnessing, or you may be passionate and prepared. It does not matter. For Jesus not only calls us to this delightful work—he also gives us the tools to carry it out.

To help readers absorb the ideas and information and put them into practice, I have included discussion questions at the end of each chapter. The questions will be helpful for both individuals and small groups that want to go deeper in learning how to speak the Good News of Jesus.

CHAPTER 1

Called to Witness

"100 million adults attend church weekly…yet the average Christian in America today will die without ever having shared their faith in Christ with another person." (George Barna Seminar, Spokane, WA, October 1998)

"Do all the witnessing you can, by all the means you can, in all the ways you can, in all the places you can, at all the times you can, to all the people you can, as long as ever…you can!" (John Wesley's rule for Christian living, modified by R. Hamel)

I only met Dima two times, and the first was at an early morning prayer meeting when he seemed barely awake. That first encounter took place at Freedom House Church in Guelph, where he was completing a summer internship. Dima refers to himself as a gypsy, a Christian Ukrainian gypsy, who grew up in Hungary. Though only in his early twenties he has visited a number of countries and has seen Christianity on the ground in various places.

On a late afternoon of a sweltering summer day, I met Dima for the second time in a Tim Hortons coffee shop. I began by asking him for his perspective on the state of the church in Canada. I have found that Christians from other countries who have had some time to observe and be a part of our church in Canada often see things with new eyes and are able to observe important details that many of us nationals are liable to miss. He thought long and hard before he answered my question, but then he began to speak.

"When I first arrived here and began to visit different churches, I was surprised, but also delighted. I was pleased to see that in the churches many of the believers knew a lot about the Bible. I was also encouraged to see much Bible knowledge among the pastors. I also discovered that there were numerous Bible colleges and seminaries. It seemed to me that there was no shortage of resources and an abundance of knowledge of basic Christian truths.

"But after being here for a short while I saw something else that greatly surprised me. I was astonished by how little the Good News of Jesus was being communicated to the wider culture. Despite much knowledge of Scripture, it seemed to me that there were few Christians doing much of anything outside of being involved in their local churches. I couldn't get over the feeling that the Good News of Jesus seemed to be stuck in the churches."

Intrigued by Dima's response, I encouraged him to go on. He did so by sharing about a conversation he had with a university student. Rob (not his real name) had confessed to Dima that he was eager to share Christ with the students

CALLED TO WITNESS

on campus and that he had actually started doing so. But he discovered that when he simply confessed to some of his fellow students that he was a Christ-follower they were shocked to the point of being "freaked out." As a result, he had backed off from any sharing about following Christ. Dima said he had encouraged Rob to keep speaking, regardless of whether people rejected him or not.

Dima also spoke of having visited many countries where it was either quasi-illegal or dangerous to openly witness about faith in Christ. Nevertheless, he noted that Christians in these countries were bravely speaking of Christ and sharing the Good News.

I confess I was not very surprised by Dima's observations, as I had noticed the same basic pattern for some time. Despite knowledge, resources, and gifting, Christians in many places in Canada seem to be comfortable in church gatherings, but few seem to have a sense of personal responsibility to take the Good News of Jesus out to a needy world.

A number of factors have contributed to this lack of witness, and we shall explore them later in this book. For now I will simply point out that Jesus has called us who follow him to come out of our church foxholes and engage with the people of a broken world, who desperately need to find abundant life in Christ.

This call to witness is modelled for us in the life of the apostle Paul. Before his conversion Paul zealously persecuted early Christians, but after meeting Jesus on the Damascus Road he became an ardent proclaimer of Jesus and embraced a new mission.

What made the difference? Simply this: Paul actually came in contact with the risen Christ. He met Christ, heard his voice, and received from him a personal commission to be "my chosen

3

instrument to carry my name before the Gentiles and their kings and before the people of Israel" (Acts 9:15).

From reading the New Testament we get the impression Paul had many experiences with Christ. The first happened at conversion, but he continued to live in communion with his Lord. Like Paul, every one of us has some kind of an "encounter" with Christ at conversion, perhaps not of the same intensity, but no less real.

After this initial meeting with Christ, we are intended to grow in deeper intimacy and closeness with him. And to the extent that we do we will tend to live in an overflowing mode. By virtue of having talked with Jesus this morning and perhaps just five minutes ago, we are ready to speak from full hearts. The secret lies in the close communion, which in turn will lead to communication. How vitally important it is for each of us to cultivate daily intimacy with Christ—for no one can share from an empty cup.

The reverse of course is also true. How is it even remotely possible to speak of Christ to a stranger, family member, or acquaintance if we have no sense of personal intimacy or closeness with Christ? If we have only a barren intellectual appreciation of who Jesus is according to correct theological doctrine, how is it possible to speak in a meaningful way about a personal relationship that barely exists?

A person may regularly attend a Christian church and be an integral part of that community and yet not have a genuine experience of salvation. Such a person will possess no desire to witness about a Christ they only know by reputation, rather than by experience. In fact, for this person the whole notion of witnessing about Christ will appear mysterious. Not possessing the inner experience of new birth by the Spirit, they will wonder why witnessing is so important. They will not necessarily be opposed, just mystified as to what they might say to someone else, because their own experience with Christ is largely an intellectual one of agreeing with the basic facts of his life, death, and resurrection.

Because of his closeness with Christ, the apostle Paul could say, "Yet I am not ashamed, because I know whom I have believed" (2 Timothy 1:12). He also wrote, "I have been crucified with Christ and I no longer live, but Christ lives in me" (Galatians 2:20). Paul did not have only an intellectual knowledge of who Christ was. He enjoyed daily a vibrant ongoing familiarity with Christ. That prepared him at the drop of a hat, whether he was on board a ship, travelling by road, or imprisoned in some dark cell, to speak of this Christ who was his constant companion.

THE BIBLICAL WITNESS ON WITNESSING

How important to Jesus was it that his disciples would bear witness? It was so crucial that he started calling them to it from the beginning; he implored them, "Come, follow me…and I will make you fishers of men" (Matthew 4:19). We see its importance when he sent out the Twelve to preach the kingdom message (Matthew 10). Furthermore, Jesus made the focus on witness one of his last in-depth teachings when he was only hours away from the cross: "You also must testify" (John 15:27). The first command Jesus gave his disciples after he rose from the dead was "As the Father has sent me, I am sending you" (John 20:21). Then we see the same focus again in his Great Commission command: "Therefore go and make disciples of all nations" (Matthew 28:19). Finally, we see it in his last words just before his ascension when he said, "But you will receive power when the Holy Spirit comes on you; and you will be my witnesses" (Acts 1:8). From beginning to end of his earthly ministry, one of Jesus' top priorities was to produce witnesses who would testify of him.

Definition of Witnessing

Witnessing may be defined as "The act of testifying by word or deed to the truth." Christians have come to use it to refer to the testimony that believers give to describe Christ's person, teaching, and saving power.

I define witnessing in the following way: "To share some aspect of the Good News of Jesus in the power of the Holy Spirit while leaving the results up to God." It is true that this is a rather broad definition of the term, but I have deliberately made it so because we witness to multiple aspects of the truth.

The vast majority of Christians down through the ages have taken for granted that Christians in every era have the same responsibility to witness as did those first eyewitness believers. But few people stop to consider that it is impossible for us today to be witnesses in exactly the same way as the disciples who walked and talked with Jesus.

Now, what do I mean by that? The apostles were, of course, eyewitnesses of Jesus' life, death, and resurrection. They walked the dusty roads of Galilee with him, ate and drank with him, and prayed with him. They witnessed the amazing miracles and heard first-hand the teachings of Jesus they later passed on. They saw him arrested, and most of them probably viewed his death, albeit from afar. They were actual eyewitnesses of his resurrection body as he sojourned with them for some forty days after rising from the tomb.

In numerous places the Scripture emphasizes that the disciples were actually with Jesus and saw him with their own eyes (Acts 1:22, 10:39, 13:31; 1 Peter 5:1, 2 Peter 1:16). But no Christian living after that era can make that same claim. This is important to consider as we think about how we are to fulfill the command to be his witnesses today.

We chiefly give testimony in two main ways. We testify to the historical truth of Jesus that we find in the Scripture. We also testify to the truth of what Jesus has done in our personal lives in granting us forgiveness of sins and coming to live within us.

To grasp and apply how we can be his witnesses today we'll look at what witnessing is and what it is not.

WHAT WITNESSING IS

First, we witness by speaking of the person and work of Jesus Christ. This does not need to be a lengthy explanation; it can be done in a passing comment. I suspect that this is the main thing that comes to the mind of most people when they hear the expression "to witness." Any expression of fact about Jesus' person—for instance, that he is the creator and sustainer of all things, the Son of God, the promised Messiah, the Saviour of the world, the one resurrected from the dead, and the one who will evaluate all our actions—is truth about Jesus and, as such, a witness to him.

Our witness could focus, as well, on some aspect of the work of Jesus. Think especially of his work of dying as a substitute for sin. Then reflect on the fact that he died not for any sin of his own, but rather for the sins of his people. His dying was planned from the very beginning of the world, came as no surprise to the Father, and forms the basis for men and women to be made acceptable with God as they put faith and trust in him.

Although we who live today have not personally seen Jesus and were not there to witness his dying, burial, and resurrection, we are able to witness to these events because they have been reported in Scripture. A historical document, the Bible, gives us a record of these truths, and we can confidently use it to help people understand who Jesus is and that what he did still blesses people.

Second, we witness by speaking of what Jesus has done in our own lives and the ways in which he has transformed us. We should note that the book of Acts has three instances in which Paul, the apostle, gives a detailed account of his personal testimony (Acts 9, 22, 26).

Third, we can witness by speaking of the teachings of Jesus. He left a rich body of teaching in the New Testament, including the Sermon on the Mount, where he taught on anger, forgiveness, lust, divorce and remarriage, heaven, and hell. We can use all of these as valid themes of witness.

For example, Jesus explicitly taught about the goodness of marriage and how it brings fundamental unity to a couple. So when one of my tennis buddies tried to get a cheap laugh from me by trashing his own marriage, I gently reproved his macho comment by saying, "Phillip [not his real name], that remark doesn't cut it with me. I've been married for thirty-eight years, and I have a wonderful wife." I think he was a little shocked. Although my comment was not lengthy, it testified to Jesus' teaching that marriage is a great good. Any time that we explain or point to what Jesus taught on any subject (anger, marriage, forgiveness, divorce, lust, etc.) we are acting as witnesses to some aspect of his teaching.

Fourth, we witness in a powerful way by living out the teaching of Jesus. We are called to live a life that is godly and righteous. We are called, after all, to walk as Jesus walked (1 John 2:6). We are under the mandate of living a life so full of good deeds that people seeing them will give glory to God (Matthew 5:16).

When a cashier mistakenly returns too much change to us and we refuse it for Christ's sake, we have spoken well by our deed. When people see us as Christians going out of our way to welcome new people in our private club, they will take note that we live differently than most. Richard Bond wrote, "As God personally brought the Good News to mankind, so we are to 'incarnate' Christ to the lost, that is, to penetrate, (pitch our tent) significantly into the lives of the non-Christian for the purpose of not only verbalizing the Gospel but also to live it before them."[1]

WHAT WITNESSING IS NOT

Witnessing is not an option. But I think that in many churches perhaps the majority of believers do not see witnessing as part of their calling. I suspect they would give a number of reasons why they think that way. I think that number one on that list would be fear, and number two would be the lack of knowledge of where to begin. I have no desire to be harsh or unsympathetic, but the Bible is crystal clear that those who believe in Jesus will speak of him.

To witness effectively does not mean that we have to present the full Good News on every occasion. We might wish that we could tell people the whole story of Jesus every time we witness, but a full presentation is more the exception than the rule. Many situations simply don't lend themselves to long conversations. For example, when we're talking with a bank clerk and people are lined up behind us waiting their turn, this should not be seen as a good opportunity for a long conversation about Christ.

But what if we were to change our understanding about what constitutes witnessing? What if we were to come to see it as any word or action that leads a person one step closer to Christ? Chris Castaldo explains this incremental type of sharing when he says,

I don't know about you, but most of my gospel encounters don't allow for a full-orbed sermon. In a crusade, the goal of the evangelist is to clearly present the entire message and urge someone to make a decision.... However, if you define all evangelism that way, what happens when you have only two minutes to talk to a colleague beside the water cooler during break? How do you witness to the checkout person in the supermarket, or to a family member who knows what you believe and is utterly disinterested in hearing any more sermons? The answer is—you don't. You don't say a thing. We can't share in that kind of way without alienating people; therefore, we don't share at all. The outcome is the same as hiding our lamps beneath the proverbial table. What we need to learn is how to gradually plant seeds of gospel truth that help people incrementally move one step closer to Christ.[2]

Even in the case of established relationships, a brief word of witness over a period of time will often be more productive than a lengthy download of Bible content. In his useful video series *Just Walk Across the Room,* Bill Hybels tells the story of Dave, whom he met when he took up competitive sailboat racing. Over a period of seven years in an ever deepening friendship Bill had many conversations with Dave in which gospel seed was planted. And finally the day came when Dave surrendered to Christ.

Someone does not have to be converted on the spot for witnessing to be considered successful. Rather, we might conceive of effective witnessing as "going fishing." Sometimes we go fishing and don't catch any fish. But does that mean we were not fishing? No, only that in that instance we didn't catch any fish. But we still had a line or a net in the water—we were still fishing.

Another image that comes to mind is sowing seed. Witnessing can be compared to dropping seeds in soil. Some seeds will be watered and cultivated, by others or by ourselves. And in due course one day we can expect a harvest. However, just because we do not harvest every time we witness does not mean that we have not been effective.

Witnessing effectively also does not mean that people have to accept us and our words. Even when we speak the truth about Christ in love, a person with a secular mindset may not welcome us. We remember that on many occasions Paul, the fearless apostle, was not accepted or his words appreciated. When Paul and Silas were beaten and thrown into jail at Philippi, it seemed that their attempts at witnessing had failed. Yet in God's providence their being jailed led to the conversion of their jailer and the beginning of a new church in that area.

We, too, as we faithfully witness even in hostile circumstances, can be confident that our work will not be lost. Neither immediate harvest nor warm acceptance by those who hear is the ultimate test. Faithfulness, the actual "going fishing," and leaving the results in God's hands is the definition of successful witnessing.

MANY WAYS TO WITNESS

Believers in Christ can witness in many different ways, in many different places, with a great variety of distinct approaches and tools. We can approach strangers in public settings or limit ourselves to that special group of people with whom we already have a tight bond. We can also focus on developing home groups where a Christianity 101 study is taught or on an Alpha course that might be taught in a church building. We can join social clubs, sports clubs, book clubs, or any kind of group that holds some interest for us. Those with a quieter bent could invite over a neighbour, write a letter to the editor of the local paper that will witness to some truth of the gospel, or find useful articles that contain some aspect of the Good News and casually give them to friends and neighbours.

Some Christians witness using creatively assertive tactics. For instance, at sporting events, like football or baseball games, some believers hold up huge placards with "John 3:16" written in large letters. Certain athletes are adept at drawing attention to the gospel. Tim Tebow, former quarterback of the Denver Broncos, often sports this same Scripture reference, John 3:16, on his face just below his eyes.[3] And right after he completes a touchdown or throws an amazing pass, he briefly drops to one knee to bow in a moment of silent prayer. This behaviour naturally catches the attention of TV commentators and sportscasters, and not always in a friendly way. However, millions of viewers have been to some degree exposed to the gospel. After one game during which Tebow displayed the "John 3:16" reference, 62 million viewers performed Internet searches using the Google search engine to try to find out what he meant by the reference.[4]

Not all Christians are comfortable with Tebow's very public and flamboyant style of witness. Yet people who do such things are attempting to follow God's leading, and we should be gentle with our criticism. They do challenge us to think in new ways, and perhaps their unusual witness raises questions as to how we ourselves might engage in some kind of public witness.

WITNESSING IS AN EVERYDAY AFFAIR
Recently some friends of ours moved into our city. Wayne and Brenda have joyfully adopted a new way of thinking as they

look forward to their new life in a fresh city. They are constantly looking for opportunities to witness. They have reminded me several times, "Every time we step out the door, we are on mission for God." For them witnessing is an everyday affair. I have no doubt that God will bless their outward looking vision. Many of us need to put on a new set of glasses that will help us to see life from an outward-focused perspective.

One aspect of witnessing, sometimes overlooked, is simply to openly confess to people that we are followers of Christ. The Bible states, "Whoever acknowledges me before men, I will also acknowledge him before my Father in heaven" (Matthew 10:32). If we have no time or opportunity to speak fully of his teaching or the meaning of his death, merely confessing his name can be a significant form of witness. This will be explored more fully later on in this book, but there are usually some moments in every single day in which we can acknowledge Christ before men. For example, if the cashier at the gas station is surprised that you are not angry like other clients because the car wash is broken, you have a wonderful opportunity to speak. Why not grab the moment and say something like "Well, Jesus teaches me to live like that. He calls me to control my anger, so he gets the credit, for I follow him."

You can see that this is not complicated at all. However, it does call for a particular mindset. We must, like Wayne and Brenda, always see ourselves on mission. If we fail to keep this in mind we will likely miss the opportunity when it is before us.

EMPOWERED TO FULFILL OUR CALLING

How is it even possible to carry out our mission? Where does the power come from? Jesus knew that the mission he had given to the disciples could not be carried out without power. And in Luke 24:46–49 and Acts 1:8, Jesus clearly taught that they would be able to fulfill their mission to be witnesses only by the energy of the promised Holy Spirit.

Nothing has changed. Today we still need the power of the Holy Spirit to fulfill this mission. And God still makes his same holy, ancient, beautiful, power of powers available to everyone. Because of this every follower of Jesus can give an unqualified "yes" to the delightful duty of talking the walk. Every one of us sheep who follow our amazing Shepherd will have no lack of resources. We will receive power to live unmuzzled lives, power "that you may declare the praises of him who called you out of darkness into his wonderful light" (1 Peter 2:9). Later on we will examine more fully the nature of this power and how we receive it.

Why don't we witness, even though we know Jesus has called us to do so and provides us with power to do it well? The delightful duty of witnessing has taken on a lot of baggage that greatly hinders our simple obedience to the task.

QUESTIONS FOR GROUP DISCUSSION

1. The apostle Paul models for us a life in which there is a close intimacy with Christ. How important to our own witnessing attempts is having this kind of close relationship? How can this be cultivated and deepened?

2. Some might argue that witnessing is not stressed that much in the New Testament. Would you agree with that position, or do you see it differently? Why or why not?

3. Are we called to be witnesses today in exactly the same way that the apostles were called? Share in your group the two main ways that we are to focus on giving witness to our own society.

4. Many people think that an opportunity for witnessing doesn't count unless the truth of the substitutionary atonement is

presented. Are they correct, or do they need to expand their understanding of what it means to witness?

5. The early believers needed the power of the Holy Spirit to carry out the command to witness. In what way do believers of today need to appropriate this same power in order to be faithful to Christ?

CHAPTER 2

Liberating Ourselves from False Concepts, Part 1

"I find that almost everyone I have ever talked with has been willing and often eager to talk about spiritual things if he can do it in a relaxed, nonthreatening situation." (Leighton Ford)

"Living a God-pleasing life is a powerful witness to the Gospel we proclaim, but it is not the Gospel. The Gospel is more than just "living out the Gospel," "practicing the Gospel" or "becoming the Gospel to our neighbors." The Gospel is primarily the message about a historical event and person, JESUS." (Dr. T.V. Thomas)

For the Christian church of our time, *witnessing* has almost become a dirty word. Just hearing the word makes many believers want to hide. Evangelist Greg

Laurie laments that Christians and unbelievers have one thing in common—they are both uptight about evangelism.[1] It is perhaps not surprising that people outside the church would be uptight about evangelism, but for Christians to feel the same way is astonishing and more than a little sad.

After all, Scripture is remarkably straightforward on this topic. The Bible explicitly teaches that all followers of Jesus would be his witnesses (Acts 1:8; Matthew 28:18–20; 2 Corinthians 5:18–20). Since the Bible and the tradition passed down to us are so clear, we might well wonder what has caused witnessing to have such a negative reputation.

Many Christians have faulty ideas about witnessing. The danger of such ideas lies in their power to deflect us from carrying out our mission. To lay a foundation for a way forward, we will examine five erroneous ideas about the nature of witnessing itself. In the next chapter we will focus on false concepts about the person who is carrying out the witnessing.

MISCONCEPTION 1: WITNESSING IS LIKE SALES

Many people think of witnessing as akin to making a sale. Upon mastering a basic idea of your product (salvation), you seek out strangers, family members, or friends and perform a fast, one-sided presentation of truth, and then push for commitment. If you are successful in buttonholing someone for as long as it takes to get them to pray a "sinner's prayer," you supposedly have done well.

Sometimes Christians have been assured that this "sales" approach requires only minimal preparation, since God will give us what we need in the moment, despite a lack of preparation. If this description is even close to what many people picture as *witnessing*, it is no wonder that a good many find themselves uptight.

Some Christians have formed their impression of witnessing from visits by some cults that use aggressive tactics to engage people in conversation. Such groups relentlessly employ assertive door-to-door sales methods to recruit new members. At a gut level we know how the average person feels about this type of pushiness, for we know how it makes us feel. We feel repelled by such tactics because they seem to lack graciousness. Even if this type of pushiness brings results, we want a better way. There is good news for all of us—there are better ways of sharing the "Good News" of Jesus.

Misconception 2: Witnessing Does Not Require Words
More than a few Christians today believe they can be "silent Christians for Christ." They argue that they can witness effectively without speaking about their faith to non-believers. So they seek as their goal to simply live out their faith day by day. They believe that people who see a genuine faith in action will ask questions, and then they can talk about their beliefs.

The claim that "walking the talk is enough" is not new. More than forty years ago I talked about it with a godly young woman I was trying to woo. She belonged to an aggressively evangelizing fundamentalist denomination yet, suprisingly, had this notion that she did not need to speak of Christ.

Not that long ago I had almost an identical conversation with another follower of Christ. She, like my friend of many years ago, had also imbibed the belief that our only duty in witnessing is to live out our faith in front of other people.

I don't want anyone to misunderstand. People who think like this are stressing a vital truth. It is crucial that we who believe in Christ and the truth of his words should demonstrate that truth by our actions. Nothing is more necessary—actions must back up our words (Matthew 5:16).

Actions alone, however, will never be enough. Unbelievers who see Christians performing good deeds are likely to conclude, "What a nice guy; what an impressive character!" Instead of Christ getting glory, we as individuals are likely to receive honour. Actions alone simply do not pass along enough information.

Furthermore, the Scripture calls us to be a speaking people. We are called over and over again to be a people who speak and confess, called to be a people who "proclaim the excellencies" of Christ (1 Peter 2:9, NASB). The two concepts of a "lived out faith" and a "spoken faith" should never be put in opposition to one another. They should always be held together. This is one of those cases where both/and must be applied.

MISCONCEPTION 3: WITNESSING IS NOT COOL, SO WE SHOULD COOL IT

Many in the public square do not welcome Christianity. Movies, for example, regularly portray Christians in highly unflattering ways. Some examples include *Saved, Priest, Dogma, The Magdalene Sisters, The Basketball Diaries,* and *Heaven Help Us.* Don Feder explores this antagonism in further detail in his excellent article "Why Hollywood Hates Christianity."[2] I suspect we believers have been more influenced than we know by such images—indeed, we are wary and guarded about how people view us.

Some believers have concluded that it simply makes sense to keep our heads down when we are in public view. During a conversation on why Christians seldom defend biblical values by writing to local newspapers, a pastor said, "I think many of us simply do not want to take those kinds of pains and for our efforts get vilified by the other side."

Margaret Atwood, a Canadian literary icon, in her book *Bluebeard's Egg* compares people who speak openly about their faith to a "flasher." She describes a flasher as an old man in a raincoat, with nothing else underneath, who furtively waits his opportunity and then shocks the person he's conversing with by opening wide his raincoat.[3] Her perception is that religious talk is supposed to be private talk. You don't just "flash it" openly in front of people you hardly know.

Certainly when we witness we should approach people with cultural sensitivity and not, as it were, furtively sneak up and pounce with the Good News. This approach lacks graciousness, and our listeners are unlikely to offer us a second opportunity to speak into their lives.

I think that Atwood is not just rejecting boorish behaviour but also reflecting something deeper. Our culture has a strong mindset that religion belongs in the private realm and it is simply not "correct practise" to speak openly about personal faith.

So should we Christians take note and stop talking about faith, since it is not culturally chic to do so? "What would Jesus do?" Did he personally model speaking his Good News publicly, even when his message was not politically correct? We see him for instance healing people on the Sabbath day and teaching that it was okay to do so (Luke 6:6–11). We see him casting out the moneychangers from the temple and condemning their actions even though they were approved by the authorities (John 2:12–16). We see him ignoring cultural mores when he spoke to the Samaritan woman and offered her the gift of life (John 4:7–26). Jesus simply did not back down—he was not silenced out of respect for the cultural norms of the day.

A more biblical and rational approach is to understand that some unbelievers have always objected to being confronted with the gospel. Some people rejected the gospel in the time of Christ. Others have done so in every generation since then. But just because sharing openly is not cool is no reason at all to back away from our obedience to Christ.

MISCONCEPTION 4: WITNESSES ARE NEVER AFRAID

Feeling some fear is normal in witnessing. None of us should be surprised we feel anxious when we begin to walk this pathway of obedience. It seems that there is a basic misunderstanding. Because we know the Holy Spirit will help us in our mission to share, we might think that speaking the truth is as easy as a walk on the beach. When we feel fearful on the witnessing journey we may either wonder what's wrong with us or question why the help of the Holy Spirit did not materialize. However, if we see fear as normal, we are prepared to spiritually fight it and not be derailed from fulfilling our mission.

On at least two occasions in Paul's ministry we see hints of fear. In Corinth, Paul ran into stiff opposition. One night the Lord spoke to him in a vision and said, "Do not be afraid; keep on speaking, do not be silent. For I am with you, and no one is going to attack and harm you, because I have many people in this city" (Acts 18:9–10). This incident instructs us that it is normal for Christians today to experience times of fear and assures us that God takes care of us. God promised to be with Paul and that he would be protected. In like manner God will be with us on all our journeys.

Perhaps one of the greatest fears for people, including Christians, is for our reputation. We know that when we share openly about our relationship with Jesus some are going to judge us, slander us, and call us fools or bigots, or worse. And, even if they say nothing, we still fear how they may feel about us. Jesus spoke directly to this type of fear in Matthew 10:24–26:

> *"A student is not above his teacher, nor a servant above his master. It is enough for the student to be like his teacher,*

and the servant like his master. If the head of the house has been called Beelzebub, how much more the members of his household! So do not be afraid of them. There is nothing concealed that will not be disclosed, or hidden that will not be made known."

Beelzebub was known as the prince of the demons, and Jesus used the word as a name for Satan. Christ was teaching here that just as he was slandered and his reputation destroyed by enemies calling him the prince of the demons, so his followers can expect to be given similar treatment.

Then Jesus took the sting out of this kind of persecution by revealing how he would help followers overcome slander. When Jesus said, "So do not be afraid of them," he immediately followed it with a promise that all will be revealed in the future. Even if we should be slandered in the present time, the time is coming when the record will be set straight. It appears that Jesus expects us to combat fear of slander by ignoring the present results of slander (loss of reputation, loss of friends, loss of employment, etc.) and instead focus our mind and hearts on the promise of vindication in the future.

MISCONCEPTION 5: WITNESSING CAN BE AVOIDED IN HOSTILE CIRCUMSTANCES

Scripture teaches that those who believe in Jesus will speak openly about that relationship. Shortly after Jesus told his disciples that the Holy Spirit would testify of him, he went on to say, "And you also must testify, for you have been with me from the beginning" (John 15:27).

I find this command astonishing. He had just prophesied that people would hate the apostles even as they hated him. And he had just predicted their coming persecution. Then right after this word of warning he unapologetically commanded them to witness to him.

Acts 5 reports one example of how this played out. The apostles had been arrested and thrown into jail because they were boldly speaking of Jesus to crowds of people. But during the night an angel let them out of prison and commanded them, "Go, stand in the temple courts…and tell the people the full message of this new life" (Acts 5:20). No, the apostles were not told to flee; nor were they given permission to find a safe place. They were sent back into the midst of danger to continue witnessing.

A good example of suffering for witnessing occurred in the aftermath of the scandal surrounding the famous golfer Tiger Woods. In 2009 he was publicly exposed in a web of lies and adulteries when a number of women reported they had shared his bed. Well-known media commentator Brit Hume courageously shared an aspect of Christian faith over this incident. He publicly suggested that Tiger Woods should seek Christ for forgiveness of his sins, since he was not likely to find forgiveness in his Buddhist religion.[4] Hume's comments raised eyebrows and provoked a good deal of anger. He was scorned and vilified for daring to invoke religion, and even more for bringing Christ into the conversation.

Suffering is to be expected. More than that, suffering is to be accepted as normal. Its pain is no signal that we are doing something wrong. Its presence should be anticipated as part of the journey of obedience (2 Timothy 1:8). I can think of several employment situations where some of my non-Christian co-workers made great sport of the fact that I was a Christian and deliberately isolated me in the workplace. I was not shocked, and over time I won their respect and acceptance.

In our next chapter we will continue to explore misconceptions but with a slightly different twist, this time exploring five false concepts about the person who carries out the witnessing.

QUESTIONS FOR GROUP DISCUSSION

1. How do you feel about hard-core salesmanship witnessing techniques? Can you give examples of Christ relating to people in this way?

2. Why are aggressive witnessing techniques often not helpful when we are seeking to converse with people about Christ?

3. Some in our society today view religious faith as a private matter that should not be exposed in public. How common do you think this is, and how do you think Christians should respond to this way of thinking?

4. Is it normal to be fearful about witnessing? How can we learn to deal with this fear?

5. It appears that the apostle Paul at times was fearful. In what ways can his experience with fear be an encouragement to us?

Liberating Ourselves from False Concepts, Part II

"Evangelism is a twenty-four-hour-a-day activity for everyone. From home, to school, to work, to play, you are constantly sending out a message to those around you with your mouth and your mannerisms."
(Joseph C. Aldrich)

Over the years I've heard many Christians confidently voice mistaken ideas about why they are excused from witnessing. In this chapter, we will examine five common excuses or reasons that believers frequently offer to justify not witnessing about Christ.

EXCUSE 1: GOOD CHRISTIANS DON'T SPEND MUCH TIME WITH UNBELIEVERS

When I was a new believer and just learning to walk as a Christian, Bob, a Christian friend, told me he had a number of close non-Christian friends with whom he spent lots of time. I was shocked. I was certain he was walking on a dangerous path. I was convinced that he should not be dabbling in the company of worldly people and should flee into safe relationships with other Christians. My friend was fairly persuasive, or maybe just argumentative, but in the end neither one of us convinced the other. However, if I could talk to Bob today I would say to him, "You were right, and I was wrong."

I have heard it said many times that only two years after becoming a follower of Christ the average Christian no longer has any non-Christian friends.[1] In some cases believers were told they should drop such relationships. In other cases, newer Christians started pulling away from those outside the faith because of differences in values and interests. Perhaps most frequently, Christians simply fill up their agendas with Christian friends and activities and have no room for anybody else.

If most believers have very few relationships with unbelievers, who are they going to witness to? They could still witness to strangers and people whom they know only superficially, but that is a limited pool of people. These believers will likely view the church as safe and secure, and every now and again they, either solo or in groups, will make forays into the surrounding culture. Once there they will attempt to contact the "natives," bear witness, and then make a beeline back into the fortress of their church community.

While it's possible to bear witness in this fashion, it is not an effective model and does not resemble the pattern Jesus passed on to us. Before we examine that model in more detail, let's first look at a couple of Scriptures that are sometimes used to justify this type of Christian isolationism.

Do not be yoked together with unbelievers. For what do righteousness and wickedness have in common? Or what fellowship can light have with darkness? What harmony is there between Christ and Belial? Or what does a believer have in common with an unbeliever?... "Therefore come out from among them and be separate, says the Lord. Touch no unclean thing, and I will receive you" (2 Corinthians 6:14–17).

A literal reading of this passage without consideration of other texts could easily lead Christians to conclude they are called to isolate themselves from unbelievers. And some have reached just that conclusion. But are they right? I think not, for several reasons.

While the passage calls for separation at some level between believer and non-believer, it doesn't forbid all contact. Christians were simply not to join in every pursuit an unbelieving neighbour might find attractive. In ancient Rome, the Christians thought it immoral to go to the local coliseum to watch the horrific gladiator fights where people were murdered for entertainment. In Elizabethan England Christians didn't go to bear or bull baiting or cock fighting, which they saw as cruel. While most Christians today have no problem attending movies, the vast majority would not go with unbelieving friends to view pornographic or semi-pornographic films.

The key to applying the text is to see that a believer is not to be "yoked" with an unbeliever. Yoked implies being united together for a common purpose, such as marriage and any kind of formal business relationship. Believers should not enter into these types of relationships with unbelievers.

While a believer can and should have basic friendships with unbelievers, there is a place for caution. Believers should maintain a certain distance and guard their hearts against becoming over-committed, because this could allow a type of "yoking" to take place, even without a formal agreement. Larry Moyer, author of *Twenty-One Things God Never Said,* feels there should always be a deeper fellowship with fellow believers because of our mutual communion with Christ.[2]

Jesus, our model above all others, did not separate himself from the world but rather developed relationships with people labelled as "sinners" by Jewish religious authorities. When tax collectors and sinners came near Jesus, the Pharisees and scribes muttered, saying, "This man welcomes sinners and eats with them" (Luke 15:1–2). He spent so much time with people the religious establishment considered unsavoury that they called him a drunkard, a glutton, and a friend of sinners (Luke 7:34). Jews considered tax collectors to be traitors, the worst kind of sinner. It should catch our attention that Jesus hung out not only with sinful people but with some of the most notorious in the land.

In Jesus' era, holy men were not supposed to have anything to do with women other than their spouse, and certainly nothing to do with immoral women. However, Jesus went out of his way to speak to a loose living woman in Samaria (John 4:7–26) and allowed another woman of questionable reputation to pour perfume on his feet and wipe it off with her hair.

Jesus came to earth to save sinners. To accomplish that he needed to eat with them, drink with them, party with them, and be touched by them. He had to come all the way into their world, so that's exactly what he did.

Another important text speaks to this theme. In 1 Corinthians 5:9–10 the apostle Paul clarified that the Corinthian Christians could associate with non-Christians. "I have written you in my letter not to associate with sexually immoral people—not at all meaning the people of this world who are immoral, or the greedy and swindlers, or idolaters. In that case you would have to leave this world." Paul is making the case that Christians have a duty to deal with sinful Christians by not associating with them. However, he is careful to point out that he is not calling Christians to stop relating to those whom the Bible would deem sinful. He definitely does not want us to avoid the sinners who are still outside the kingdom. That would require us to leave the world. That is not his call for our lives.

So this passage gives the clear, positive message that we are to associate with sinners. He calls us to go where sinners live and hang out with them. In *Twenty-One Things God Never Said,* Larry Moyer underscores this truth when he says, "Fishing for men requires contacting men. Contacting men requires conversing with men…In the midst of those contacts and conversations, the gospel is shared, and people face their need for Christ."[3]

Jesus didn't do evangelism from the comfort of the fortress of heaven. He journeyed all the way into our sinful culture. He ate with us, attended our parties, and talked to us. In short, he deliberately entered our space and in the context of relationship shared the beautiful message of eternal life. He simply calls us to do the same.

EXCUSE 2: ONLY CLERGY AND SEMINARY PROFESSORS ARE CALLED TO SHARE THE FAITH

Surprisingly, some people believe that only ministers and seminary professors are called to share the faith. A church elder, and friend of mine, once insisted he had never been taught that God expects ordinary Christians to bear witness. He was sure that the command to "go into all the world" applied only to full-time clergy. The elder was content to farm and leave witnessing and evangelizing in the hands of the pastor.

There is a certain logic to the position. After all, ministers and professionals have been trained in the core truths of the faith and have an ability to talk about them that the average Christian does not have. Perhaps there is confusion because Christian professionals get paid to speak while the ordinary Christian doesn't get paid to witness or have years of seminary training to prepare him to do so.

But the deeper problem of my church elder friend is more likely related to the idea of Christian "callings," which Martin Luther highlighted in the sixteenth century. Luther brought back the biblical idea that God calls people to all kinds of occupations and spheres of work. He wanted to counteract the false idea that the work of religious professionals like priests, monks, or nuns was more holy unto God than the kind of work that farmers, blacksmiths, cooks, or bakers did.

Luther's teaching on callings served to properly elevate and sanctify all types of work. However, the teaching has led some Christians to falsely reason that since God called them to a secular calling they have no personal responsibility to witness to Christ. However, a broader understanding of Scripture leads us to conclude that God wants us all to live out our callings first and foremost as Christians. So then, whether we are doctors, taxi drivers, Internet specialists, artists or writers, we should so live that by word and deed we faithfully bear witness to the Light who has come (Matthew 5:13–16, 28:18–20, Philippians 1:27–28, 2:14–16, Colossians 4:5–6).

Actually, pastors and other religious professionals may have more barriers than lay Christians do when it comes to witnessing. People tend to be uneasy around clergy and frequently clam up when they know they are talking to a pastor. In addition, pastors frequently have little or no social life apart from relationships with fellow believers. This is not necessarily their preference but often comes with the territory.

One pastor found that his ministry of overseeing small groups in a large church took up to sixty hours a week. Sadly then, in his normal work week he simply did not have time to come in contact with unbelievers. Many in full-time Christian ministry find themselves in this bind. Pastors may have to think outside the box to ensure they have regular contact with those who need to hear the message of Jesus.

Excuse 3: Only People with the Gift of Evangelism Are Called to Share the Faith

Many Christians feel strongly that since they do not have the "gift" of evangelism listed in Ephesians 4:11–13, they are exempt from the call to witness. They may have heard a speaker say something like this and concluded that the passages in Scripture calling for Christians to witness don't apply to them.

The Ephesians passage lists various types of gifted persons Christ has given us to build up the church: apostles, prophets, evangelists, pastors, and teachers. The passage doesn't define the term "evangelist," but from its root meaning we can safely conclude that it speaks of one who has been gifted with ability and effectiveness in sharing the Good News of Christ.

Those who conclude they are excused from witnessing because they don't possess the gift of evangelism are indulging in a logical fallacy. Although God may not have gifted all of us to be evangelists, he has still called all of us to be witnesses (Acts 1:8, Matthew 28:19–20). It simply does not follow that because God has given evangelists more power, ability, and effectiveness in their witnessing, other believers are exempt from giving witness. Rather, ordinary believers should seek out evangelists and receive training from them so that they can be more effective witnesses.

However, there is a second aspect of what it means to have the gift of evangelism, which can be seen in the context. The passage says these gifted people have been given to build up the church and equip her for works of service. This includes the evangelist. Today, pastors and teachers are widely held to be the ones to fulfill the work of equipping and building up the church. Perhaps pastors, who are almost always overworked, could release and empower evangelists to carry out ongoing training.

Excuse 4: Only People Skilled in Apologetics Should Practice Witnessing

Many believers turn away from the joy and call of witnessing because they do not feel qualified to respond to difficult questions. They fear they will encounter a person who wants to debate the faith and will have nothing to say. They want to leave the task of defending the faith to those who have been trained in apologetics. Their conclusion is easy to understand.

It is true that we will from time to time have encounters with people who raise questions we cannot answer. Jesus didn't have that problem, but the rest of us will. This fear can be handled head on by using a simple technique. When someone makes an objection or a comment we are unable to answer all we need to say is, "That's a good question, and I have to admit I don't have a good response on the tip of my tongue. But, I'd like to honour your question, so if you will permit me I will look up the answer and share it with you when we meet again." For most people this will serve quite nicely as a response.

Now, don't get me wrong. I'm not saying that we shouldn't prepare to share the gospel. We should all seek to be equipped as well as possible and have basic training in how to present the gospel. Indeed, it would be good to have answers to basic objections. But if we wait until we all have all the theological answers, we are not likely to ever share anything with anybody.

In reality, most people we meet are not itching to debate. Many of them are hurting. Some are quite broken. And after they enter into conversation, many are open to hearing about the Good News of Christ. The key is to genuinely love the person, which will be evident in the courtesy and respect given.

Frequently our witnessing will not even come close to debate and objections. Generally, when the person is new to us, we will not have a deep conversation but will simply drop a few seeds of truth in a loving way. For example, a cashier in Tim Hortons whom I'd met before responded to my cheery greeting by sharing that she felt quite sick and yearned to go home. I was the only customer near the till, and I asked if I could pray for her. Astonished, she reached out to take my hand. I quickly bowed my head and prayed a prayer for her healing. Then I blessed her again and said I would keep praying for her. She was quite touched, continuing to gaze at me in astonishment as I left the store.

When I saw her two days later, she told me, "It was an amazing thing, but right after you left, my boss came out of the back, took one look at me, and insisted that I book off sick and go home immediately."

I dare to assert that when we truly love people and have the courage to express it, amazing things will happen. Theodore Roosevelt is credited with saying, "People don't care how much you know until they know how much you care."

Even the great apostle Paul was not able to always successfully answer objections and was frequently kicked out of synagogues because he was on the losing end in debates with

Jewish leadership (Acts 13:42–52, Acts 14:1–7, 19–22). In Acts 17, when he spoke to a Gentile audience he was mockingly rejected by some of his listeners. He was stoned, beaten with rods, and suffered any number of persecutions because he refused to keep quiet about Christ. He must surely rank as one of the greatest evangelists and witnesses in the history of the church—yet he did not always successfully answer the objections of his hearers.

Paul's experience demonstrates it is normal that some will object and disagree with what we say. Therefore, we should not be surprised to meet with some level of resistance when we share Christ's message. This is simply part of what it means to be a speaking Christian. Just because we do not "win" in every encounter does not mean that we have failed. Witnessing is not primarily about winning arguments but rather about sharing a message in a context of love.

EXCUSE 5: ONLY PEOPLE WHOSE TESTIMONY IS ABOVE REPROACH SHOULD SHARE

On more than one occasion I have met people who said they would like to speak openly about Christ but habitually do the opposite at work and with friends. They would not deny their faith if asked about it directly, but they do not openly confess Christ and even have a kind of logic that guides them in this behaviour.

They know just how imperfect they are as Christians and feel deeply the many mistakes they make daily. They are only too aware that they have often failed miserably as Christians with the people they work with. So they have concluded that it's better to not advertise their claim to follow Christ.

Some who think like this may well believe that it is a humble way of living and that it would be somewhat prideful to openly claim to be a follower of Christ. They may even have been taught this by an earnest parent who said that Christians must not claim too much for ourselves.

This thinking is based on a fundamental fallacy—nobody, absolutely nobody, has ever lived the Christian life without sin and mistakes, except for Jesus. Christ never anticipated that his followers would live perfect lives. The New Testament teaches that we are sinners from birth, we continue as sinners in life, and we shall die while yet imperfect. Of course we are to strive towards living holy lives and never get comfortable with our sinning, but we shall never be fully perfected in this life.

The Scripture calls us to be witnesses in spite of our imperfections. It also calls us to deal with our sin and take responsibility for it. If, for example, we sin against a co-worker by "blowing up" at them, we might say the following to them when we next meet: "You know, Jack, when I got home last night I thought about how I beat up on you with all those angry words. God has shown me that I was not right in what I said or in how I said it. And I want you to know that I'm sorry, and I'm asking you to forgive me."

The reality is that our co-workers know that we are imperfect creatures. How we handle our sin and imperfections with them is the crucial issue. When they see us acting with humility and confessing wrong, it will not damage our credibility. On the contrary! It will make them think more positively of us.

Jesus knew from the beginning that our witness of him to a watching world would have to be done through imperfect, sinful people like us. But he told us to do it anyway. Our job is to trust him. He knows what he wants—he knows what will be effective before a watching world. And when our light is dim, when it is somewhat darkened because of personal sin, he gives us a way forward.

So let us boldly and confidently confess his name. And when we stumble, let us humbly and with brokenness confess that we are imperfect followers. Let us continue confidently to point our friends to the only one who is perfect, Jesus himself.

I truly believe that the vast majority of Christians would love to become unmuzzled, gladly seizing opportunities to witness for Jesus. But many would say they do not have the power or ability to do so. In our next section we will look at where we receive this power to fulfill the will of the Shepherd, who still calls us to follow.

QUESTIONS FOR GROUP DISCUSSION

1. How significant is my claim that Christians generally do not spend much time with unbelievers? To what extent will this impact our witness to those still outside the faith?

2. Have you met fellow Christ-followers who believe that only professionals have a duty to engage in witnessing? How would you respond to their claim now, after reading this chapter?

3. It is still relatively common to hear a believer express reluctance to engage in witnessing because he or she does not have the gift of evangelism. How would you help this person to see that this does not give them a valid reason to remain silent about Christ?

4. You and I have met people who feel strongly that their testimony and level of sanctification prevent them from being witnesses to Christ. How might you encourage them to think about this in a different way that might free them to share more faithfully?

CHAPTER 4

The Power Source

*You are witnesses of these things. I am going to send you
what my Father has promised; but stay in the city until
you have been clothed with power from on high*
(Luke 24:48–49).

*But you will receive power when the Holy Spirit comes
on you; and you will be my witnesses in Jerusalem, and
in all Judea and Samaria, and to the ends of the earth*
(Acts 1:8).

A person can have a genuine love for Jesus, care about
people, learn a simple presentation of the gospel, and
encounter opportunities, but still not be effective in
witnessing. I have met Christians who assume that the energy
and power to witness will automatically come to people if
they are simply shown their responsibility to witness from

various Scripture passages, including the Great Commission in Matthew 28: 18–20. However, even a cursory study of the book of Acts reveals that both prayer and the Holy Spirit are very much linked to finding power for witness.

I experienced this in the 1970s when I took a course called Evangelism Explosion, which gave me a brilliantly simple, concise, scriptural way to share the Good News with anyone. Yet, grateful as I was for the information and the new tools, I sensed something was missing. I simply did not have the ongoing courage and drive to go out and use it. Neil Cole, who writes extensively on making disciples, says, "We assumed that it is training that is needed, but we have found that training does not overcome the barriers that keep Christians from sharing the gospel."[1]

One of those barriers is lack of power to fulfill the calling to witness. Jesus diligently taught his disciples about the power they needed for witnessing. In Acts 1:4 he commanded his apostles to stay in Jerusalem and wait for the gift (the Holy Spirit) that the Father had promised to them. They obeyed, but they did not just wait passively in an upper room; instead they "all joined together constantly in prayer" (Acts 1:14).

On the day of Pentecost the Holy Spirit fell upon them and they received power to witness. These disciples, who only a few days earlier had huddled fearfully behind locked doors, suddenly had steel injected into their spines. The muzzles that had kept them bound in silence and fear fell off, and they boldly began to speak the Good News. Immediately after the Spirit came Peter preached his famous sermon, and some 3,000 people were added to the church.

THE CONNECTION BETWEEN PRAYER AND EVANGELISM
Recently I heard Pastor Bob Penhearow of Grace Trinity Community Church say that we are preoccupied too much with

methods of evangelism and too little with prayer. I agree. It is too easy to think that methods or strategy will bring people into the kingdom of God. If we want to return to the bottom line in witnessing, we must get much more serious about prayer.

Acts 3 tells us that Peter and John were on their way to the temple to pray at three in the afternoon, indicating that the early Christians continued the Jewish habit of praying at least three times a day. At that moment, by the power of God, Peter healed a lame man. After a large crowd had gathered, Peter seized the opportunity to preach Christ, and many put faith in him. Clearly, God used the miracle of healing and the preaching to convert a large number of people—but we dare not overlook the fact that the men God chose to use happened to be on their way to a prayer meeting.

The apostles were then brought before the Jewish rulers, who commanded them to keep quiet about Jesus (Acts 4:18). But when Peter and John went back to their companions and reported all that happened, including the threats, these disciples immediately held a prayer meeting. They did not pray for protection but asked God to enable them to speak the word with great boldness (Acts 4:29). God answered their prayer: "After they prayed, the place where they were meeting was shaken. And they were all filled with the Holy Spirit and spoke the word of God boldly" (Acts 4:31).

Shortly afterwards, the Jews flogged the apostles and again told them to stop talking about Jesus. However, the apostles rejoiced they had been considered worthy of suffering for Jesus and "day after day…never stopped teaching and proclaiming [him]" (Acts 5:42). It is clear that praying people received the power to witness in spite of major obstacles.

Why should prayer be so significant to the task of witnessing? It seems that God delights to hear and respond to his people as they acknowledge their need for power. Secondly it surely is linked to the fact that God is a prayer-answering God, and he actually hears and works by his power when we ask him to effect the conversion of precious people.

But something even deeper is at work—only God himself has the power to regenerate men and women. Since he alone can do this work, we must be people who are continually calling on him to do so. We must never forget that while God does use the means of witness and prayer on our part, he alone does the actual work of bringing new people into his kingdom.

Prayer is also important because it is one of God's key strategies to prepare and shape us to fulfill his will for our lives, including witnessing. As we commune with God, he speaks to us, convicts us of sin, and leads us into embracing a fuller and deeper obedience to all of his commands.

He will also direct us. At one point when my wife, Linda, and I were serving as missionaries we came to a point of profound discouragement in our particular assignment. After thinking long and hard we agreed that we were in the wrong place. But before making definite plans to leave we decided to seriously pray for an extended period, seeking God for definite guidance in this difficult decision. At the end of that time, much to our astonishment, God had specifically spoken the same message to both of us. God's plan was different from ours. He wanted us to stay the course.

In the eighteenth century, a small, relatively obscure group of people accomplished some amazing things for God because they prayed. The Moravians had fled from persecution during religious wars and found safe haven on an estate in what is now Germany. In time, under the leadership of Count von Zinzendorf, they grew spiritually in remarkable ways. Specifically, they came to greatly treasure Christ and sought ardently to obey him. Though small in number they sent out missionaries to many countries and successfully planted many churches.

The Moravian Christians seriously prayed. They believed the fire of prayer before the altar should never be allowed to go out. On August 27, 1727, twenty-four men and twenty-four women made a solemn covenant to pray for one hour a day.[2] They began faithfully praying around the clock, instituting a prayer movement that lasted more than a hundred years. Six months after the praying began, the Moravian leaders sent missionaries to the West Indies, Greenland, Turkey, and Lapland. Within sixty-five years the Moravians had sent out some 300 missionaries.[3]

THE CONNECTION BETWEEN THE HOLY SPIRIT AND EVANGELISM

Both the book of Acts and the words of Jesus in Luke 24 make it clear that a direct link exists between the work of the Holy Spirit and the task of witnessing. Specifically, Acts 1:8 and Luke 24:49 indicate that power will be given to the believer as a result of the work of the Holy Spirit.

However, some today wonder whether the coming of the Holy Spirit to the early disciples is just interesting biblical history or if it holds promise for us today. In his sermon that day Peter, speaking of the Holy Spirit, said, "The promise is for you and your children and for all who are far off—for all whom the Lord our God will call" (Acts 2:39). He made it clear that the promised Holy Spirit, who brings power to witness (Acts 1:8), is available to the followers of Christ today.

Yet many commentators, pastors, and authors seem to ignore this linkage. Some maintain that the apostles were filled with boldness and power to witness because they had seen Jesus raised up from the dead. They reason that his resurrection appearances sent the apostles forth, speaking of Christ with enthusiasm and confidence. They ignore the fact that the apostles did nothing of the sort until ten days had passed while they waited for the promised Holy Spirit. Only then did they speak with courage and an intrepid spirit (Acts 2).

Others insist that the apostles were so convinced Jesus would return soon and were so excited about it that they could not keep quiet about him. However, this view overlooks a crucial fact—the disciples kept their excitement to themselves until the Holy Spirit came.

Jesus Prioritizes the Work of the Holy Spirit

Jesus laid much stress on the importance of the Holy Spirit in providing power for the work of witnessing. When Jesus appeared to the gathered disciples in the evening of the day of resurrection, he gave them their first missionary mandate by saying, "Peace be with you! As the Father has sent me, I am sending you." Then he breathed on them and said, "Receive the Holy Spirit" (John 20:21–22). In his commentary, Matthew Henry sees this imparting of the Spirit as an earnest of the fuller impartation that they would receive not many days in the future on the day of Pentecost.[4] Jesus knew that as the apostles went out into mission they would need the power of the Holy Spirit to carry out their work.

In a passage similar to the Great Commission in Matthew 28:19–20, Jesus told the disciples to wait in Jerusalem until they had been clothed with power from on high (Luke 24:45–49). In the context it is obvious that he is referring to their receiving power to carry out their mission of evangelism and witnessing. This command to wait is repeated in Acts 1:5–8, where we see Jesus prophesying that power will be given and they will be witnesses starting in Jerusalem and extending to the ends of the earth.

As witness is carried out, the Spirit works courage in the life of the believer, but the Spirit also has a special work of bringing conviction to the unbeliever. Just how does the Holy Spirit perform the work of bringing this conviction? John 16:8 makes it plain that when the Spirit comes "he will convict the world of guilt in regard to sin and righteousness and judgment." We need to understand that this conviction normally will be personal, by virtue of the believer being in contact with the unbeliever, since the Spirit inhabits the believer.

We do not have a picture here of the Holy Spirit convicting of sin in a general fashion, as though he were a fog or a mist blanketing a city. As the believer interacts with the unbeliever, the Holy Spirit, indwelling the believer, will bring about awareness of sin in various ways. This does not mean that the Spirit cannot act independently of the believer. But it does mean that realization of sin usually occurs as the believer is in close contact with the unbeliever.

We see examples of this occurring in Scripture when Peter preached to unbelievers at Pentecost and later in the house of Cornelius. Many were convicted of sin and were converted (Acts 2:37, Acts 10:47). We see it happen to the Ethiopian eunuch as he read Scripture and conversed with Philip (Acts 8). Finally, we see it when Jesus directly confronted sin (John 4:6–19, 29). It is important for us to see the truth of this point because God's normal way of bringing conviction of sin is by having believers who have the Spirit (all believers by definition) come alongside those who are not part of Christ's kingdom.

The Holy Spirit Comes with Great Impact
When the Holy Spirit fell on the disciples on the day of Pentecost, the result was the immediate proclamation of Jesus as Lord (Acts 2:14–41), with some 3,000 people being baptized

that day. A short time later, as a result of Peter's second sermon, the number of men increased to about 5,000 (Acts 4:4).

The special work of the Spirit in empowering for witness did not end with the day of Pentecost. F. F. Bruce notes that when Peter and John were brought before the Sanhedrin to answer for their actions in preaching about Jesus, Peter received special inspiration from the Holy Spirit for this immediate need.[5] The New International Version simply says that Peter was filled with the Holy Spirit.

Here we observe that at times the phrase "filled with the spirit" can refer to an abiding character quality, such as when Stephen's character is described (Acts 6:5). However, it can also refer to the immediate and special empowerment of the Holy Spirit, as happened to the apostles in Acts 4:31 when they needed courage to keep witnessing in the face of persecution.

The Holy Spirit imparted the same power to the Moravians. In August of 1727, the Moravian believers in Herrnhut, Germany, were in the midst of intense squabbling and disagreements. Then, in an amazing worship service on August 13th, the Holy Spirit descended in a powerful way, melting the hearts of all, creating a deep oneness of purpose that simply did not exist before.[6] Beyond that, the Spirit gave them a deeper illumination of who Christ was and what he had done for them and inspired them with a new love for him. As a direct result, the Moravians experienced a new desire to take the gospel to people who had never heard it before. The Moravians always looked back to that moment as a special filling of the Holy Spirit, which prepared them to go forth boldly with the Good News of Jesus.

It reminds me of the words of the apostle Paul when he was giving his defense in front of King Agrippa, "Therefore, having obtained help from God, to this day I stand, witnessing both to small and great" (Acts 26:22 NKJV).

The Spirit has given what appears to be a filling of special power to believers on many other occasions. We could cite the First Great Awakening under the preaching of Jonathan Edwards and George Whitefield. We could speak of Andrew Murray and the revival that broke out in South Africa or of the amazing work of the Spirit that came to the early Methodists and caused them to be powerful evangelists throughout much of England and the United States. The bottom line is that special fillings are almost always associated with the giving of passion and power to witness and evangelize.

The Holy Spirit Still Gives Power for Witness

A personal experience demonstrates that the power of the Holy Spirit is still available to us. About three years ago, I was in a prayer meeting when a friend and I were particularly burdened with the need to have the Holy Spirit give us power to witness more boldly. So we prayed repeatedly and with an unusual sense of longing that he would give us that power and zeal.

Nothing out of the ordinary seemed to happen, the prayer meeting ended, and we all went our separate ways. On the way home I went into a convenience store to buy milk. As I was walking out I sensed God's Spirit calling me back to speak to the cashier.

I started a conversation with the earnest young man about spiritual things, and God gave me a brief but fascinating time of sharing faith. Since then I have talked with him, a Muslim, a number of times. Once he brought up the topic of Christ before I had a chance to do so.

In the days that followed, I found myself praying frequently. I was especially conscious of wanting to speak of Christ and to bring honour to him. Regardless of what I was doing, I found myself almost constantly in a spirit of prayer, especially desirous of having power and opportunities to witness. I didn't have to force myself to live in that spirit of prayer; it seemed rather that the Spirit was continually nudging me to seek after God and his power to witness.

A few days later, on Sunday morning, I was drinking coffee in a local Tim Hortons when a man I had been trying to get to know better walked in. Jeremy (not his real name) worked as a bouncer in a nightclub. In spite of his bald head and great size, I thought of him as a gentle giant. As we had coffee together we spoke about many things, none of them spiritual, but I sensed that the Spirit was leading me. I felt privileged to begin to build a relationship with him. I was confident that I would see him again.

That afternoon I went for a bike ride with a bag of tracts (Christian pamphlets) slung over my shoulder. On my ride through a park I encountered a tiny toddler walking down the path the wrong way. I dismounted and discovered his mom and dad were close by. Upon exchanging greetings, I detected they were Hispanic, and just for the fun of practicing my Spanish I struck up a conversation. I shared with them that I was a Christ-follower and gave them a relevant tract. They gave me an email address so I could contact them. The whole conversation was very natural, in fact highly comfortable, and I sensed that the Spirit was leading me on.

I continued on but soon had to stop to wait my turn to cross the river. I gave right of way to a tattooed young man wearing a T-shirt with a cross on it. I called out to him, asking about the cross. It turned out that it was not a cross after all, just an artistic "T." But now I had his attention. After he heard I was a Christ-follower he graciously accepted my tract and warmly said he would read it and take it under advisement.

I was astonished, for I had rarely had so many opportunities to witness in such a short time. I biked on, continuing to pray, seeking to be open to whomever the Spirit would guide me to.

Farther down the path I stopped to talk with an eighty-six-year-old man I had met before. At one point he said, "My father taught me to respect the Almighty, but he also taught me that the church was not worthy of respect." I got a little defensive but continued talking and in the end offered him a tract. He assured me he would read it. I suspected we would meet again, for he was open to talk more.

While taking a break at a Tim Hortons at the end of the trail, I met a cashier who hailed from Afghanistan. We talked about his name, for I wanted to make sure I had pronounced it correctly. Then I asked him about the book, *The Kite Runner* (a story centred in Afghanistan); he assured me he had read and enjoyed it. When I told him I had written an article about the book he seemed interested and wondered if he could get a copy. On my next visit to that Tim Hortons I made sure I had a copy, because the gospel, in part, is revealed in the article. I learned later the cashier read it and gave it to his father to read as well.

While I was praising God for my encounters, I realized that it was time I got home. However, on the trail back to my house I saw a man I had greeted earlier. He recognized me and seemed interested in talking. So I got off my bike, and we started chatting. I asked him if he was walking to take off weight. This opened a conversation about his struggle with weight loss. We talked freely, and I told him I was a Christ-follower and gave him a tract, which he willingly received. He gave me his business card and encouraged me to email him and talk to him at any time. Then I got on my bike once more and headed for home.

I miss many chances to witness and do not consider myself any great expert, but I have learned that one factor keeping many of us from witnessing is that we make it too complicated. We think that witnessing has to be a full verbal presentation of the substitutionary atonement. Obviously, it is wonderful when God opens a door for such a comprehensive sharing. However, in the meantime, vast numbers of people need desperately some seed of gospel witness to fall into their lives. What God enabled me to do by his Spirit on that Sunday afternoon was not complicated. It was a seed-planting afternoon. Other people will water, others will cultivate the ground, and still others will bring in the harvest. Everyone has a part to play.

I was radically changed. Whenever I leave my house to go anywhere I am always looking for opportunities to witness for Christ. In reality, those opportunities are happening with much greater frequency than before. Not long ago I said to my wife, "Sometimes I wonder if I'm just kidding myself. I wonder if it's really that different."

She bluntly responded, "All I know is that my husband used to go for walks and come home; he still goes for walks, but now he's always coming home with stories of how he had a chance to witness. Yes, things really are different."

I wonder what would happen if we, every day, simply recognized the place of the Holy Spirit in giving power to witness. Every day when our feet hit the floor in the morning and every time we are in a group praying, let's ask for the promised power of the Holy Spirit to fulfill the mission given to us by our Shepherd.

Having the power to speak and give witness to the truth doesn't mean we don't have to prepare in order to witness well. In the next section we shall discuss why it is so important that we equip ourselves to share the gospel of Jesus.

QUESTIONS FOR GROUP DISCUSSION

1. Excellent methods of training in witnessing are available and very important. But are they sufficient in themselves? Discuss what other factors are needed to help us get us off our couches and send us into the world to share our faith.

2. How important was prayer for the early Christians as they sought to engage in witnessing? How might we structure our lives differently in order to find time to pray consistently?

3. What role did the Holy Spirit have in the life of the early church that helped them go forward in evangelism and witness? What implications do your answers have for you today as you seek to be someone who naturally shares Christ?

CHAPTER 5

The Content of Our Witness

"A gospel which merely says, 'Come to Jesus' and offers him as a friend, and offers a marvellous new life without convincing of sin, is not New Testament evangelism…True evangelism must always start by preaching the law." (Martyn Lloyd-Jones)

"I consider that the chief dangers which confront the coming century will be religion without the Holy Ghost; Christianity without Christ; forgiveness without repentance; salvation without regeneration; politics without God; and Heaven without Hell." (General William Booth)

When Jesus told his first followers that they would be witnesses, what were they supposed to say about him in Jerusalem, Judea, Samaria, and to the ends of the earth? What did Jesus mean by the prophecy that they would be his witnesses (Acts 1:8)? What is the substance of the content that we are called to share with those who do not know Christ?

The answer to these questions is found in the last conversation that Jesus had with his disciples. On this very last occasion just before he ascended to the Father he said,

> *"This is what is written: The Christ will suffer and rise from the dead on the third day, and repentance and forgiveness of sins will be preached in his name to all nations, beginning at Jerusalem. You are witnesses of these things. I am going to send you what my Father has promised; but stay in the city until you have been clothed with power from on high"* (Luke 24:46–49).

In a few brief sentences Jesus laid out the core of the Good News. He, the Messiah, had suffered and died and risen again on the third day, and because of that repentance for the forgiveness of sins was to be preached to all nations.

Another key passage discussing the content of Christian witness is remarkably similar to the passage in Luke 24. In 1 Corinthians 15:1–6 Paul writes,

> *Now, brothers, I want to remind you of the gospel I preached to you, which you received and on which you have taken your stand. By this gospel you are saved, if you hold firmly to the word I preached to you. Otherwise, you have believed in vain.*
> *For what I received I passed on to you as of first importance: that Christ died for our sins according to the Scriptures,*

that he was buried, that he was raised on the third day according to the Scriptures, and that he appeared to Peter and then to the Twelve. After that, he appeared to more than five hundred of the brothers at the same time, most of whom are still living, though some have fallen asleep.

This passage is especially significant, for Paul implies that he is laying out the key elements in the gospel. Furthermore, he indicates that what he had passed on in his teaching was "of first importance."

Jesus is Fully God and Perfectly Man

When we witness we are to begin with the person of Jesus. He is part of the Godhead, the second person of that Trinity, and is co-equal with the Father and the Holy Spirit. As God, he has existed from all eternity, having no beginning and no ending.

The Bible speaks of God as being the powerful creator of all things, but in other places it specifically names Jesus as being the author of all (Hebrews 1:2). It appears that the Father used Jesus as his agent to bring all of creation into being. Yes, Jesus is the one who pasted all the stars and planets of the universe into their proper places.

But Jesus, in some mysterious way that we humans cannot fathom, left for a time his place with the Father in heaven and came to earth to take on human nature. He became perfectly human, with a fully formed human nature and body. Although fully human, he nevertheless is different from all other persons because he is the only one in the history of the world who never sinned. It is this fact that makes him a person who can be safely followed and emulated. Many in our present secularized society are willing to accept Jesus as a good man but find it difficult to accept his divinity. But the Scripture does not allow that interpretation. Over and over again Jesus is clearly presented as divine (John 1:1, Hebrews 1:1–4, Romans 9:5, Colossians 2:9).

Jesus was raised by Joseph and Mary and lived an unremarkable life up to about the age of thirty. Then he began his ministry of teaching, preaching, and performing miracles. The remarkable miracles of healing and casting out demons greatly ministered to sick and oppressed people. But even more, these same miracles demonstrated his credentials as the promised Messiah whom the Jewish people had been awaiting for centuries.

Nevertheless, the Jews rejected Jesus and delivered him to the Romans to be crucified. He suffered an excruciating flogging before the soldiers cruelly nailed him to the cross. After his death, his friends came and buried him in a garden tomb.

On the third day after his death, he rose from the dead, to the amazement of his followers and the consternation of his enemies. During the next forty days he repeatedly appeared to his disciples. After that, he ascended into the heavens, where he now sits at the right hand of God the Father.

These thoughts do not exhaust the things that could be said about Jesus, but they do outline the basic truths we want to share with non-believers. Whenever we bring up any of these points we bear witness for Jesus and to him by pointing to him.

THE MEANING OF JESUS' DEATH AND RESURRECTION

When we witness for Jesus we often need to explain what the basic truths of his existence and actions mean. Nowhere does this take on more importance than when we discuss his bloody death on the cross. We need to point to the substitutionary nature of Jesus' death, that his death was not in payment for his own sins (he had no sin), but rather that he died to pay for the sins of others. We need to explicitly teach that God's wrath against sin was poured out on Jesus, who thus died as a substitute for us. Then we need to teach that those who believe in Jesus as Saviour and Lord receive the amazing gift of an ongoing relationship with the Father whose love has been poured out upon them.

It is hard to overstate the importance of the resurrection of Jesus. Since Jesus had predicted it would come to pass, it proves that his words can be trusted. The resurrection also demonstrates that our own resurrection as believers is highly plausible, since Jesus has already gone through the dark tunnel of death successfully and has come out on the other side.

The news that we can come back from the dead surprises some people, like Jesse, whom I met at the gym one day. Jesse is a talkative, funny, flippant kind of person with an engaging personality. One day we were talking about getting older and the aches and pains that come with the territory. I said that when all was said and done, the ravages of age were certainly a lot better than the alternative. Jesse flippantly agreed and went on to say, "That's for sure. The one thing we know for certain is that nobody has ever come back from the dead; when you're gone, you're gone."

Before I could stop myself, I blurted out, "But that's not true! Someone did come back from the dead."

"Who?"

"Jesus," I said.

My friend's face fell, and he looked a little nonplussed but gamely responded, "Well, I suppose that's true, if you happen to believe in that sort of thing."

I had not been thinking of witnessing at all. But in the flow of conversation I was presented with the option of either denying what happened to Jesus or affirming that someone really did rise from the dead.

Having come to know my friend a little better I suspect there are few, if any, people in his life who will remind him that Jesus is one who came back from the dead. Even if people outside the faith reject this fundamental Christian truth, it is important that they meet people who believe it and are willing to affirm it.

JESUS CALLS PEOPLE TO FAITH AND REPENTANCE

The themes of faith and repentance, which are woven throughout the pages of the New Testament, are hugely important teachings we must not overlook as we share the Good News with lost people. Sadly, it is all too possible for people to have merely an intellectual grasp of the Good News and to never have entered into eternal life for want of exercising both repentance and faith. I believe that nominal or name-only Christianity often starts at this very point. Many, many understand the basic facts about Jesus and why he came and essentially affirm correct teaching. But merely to affirm one's belief in the facts of the faith is not enough.

From beginning to end, the New Testament teaches the crucial role of faith. Very early in Jesus' ministry a Pharisee named Nicodemus approached him, anxiously wanting to know what he had to do to be sure of eternal life. During their conversation Jesus said plainly that the Son of Man must be lifted up, "that everyone who believes in him may have eternal life" (John 3:15).

In the early part of Romans (1:16–17), Paul speaks of not being ashamed of the gospel, precisely because belief or faith in it brings salvation. In John 6:28–29, when Jesus speaks of the kind of work that is acceptable to God, it turns out that it is faith, not work as we would understand it. Jesus says, "The work of God is this: to believe in the one he has sent." In Hebrews

11, the Bible says we cannot please God apart from faith. And finally in Romans 5:1, Paul says we cannot be justified (made righteous) apart from faith.

Faith is simply reaching out to God to receive from him the salvation that he has made available in Jesus. By faith, we personally put trust in Jesus alone as the one who saves us from the guilt and condemnation of our sin. By faith, we personally put our trust in Jesus as the doorway to knowing God and discover as well that he is the doorway by which one day we will be ushered into heaven.

When talking to people about how faith operates I often use an empty chair as a vivid illustration. I tell them, "That empty chair looks strong enough to bear my weight, but unless I actually lower myself onto it and allow it to take all of my weight I will never know for sure. I must personally express my trust in its strength by actually sitting in it. Until I do that it will not be a help or any kind of comfort to me. In a similar way we must personally place trust in Christ by 'sitting down' and resting on the truth that he died so that our sins might be blotted out."

Repentance

Paul modelled in his preaching that repentance is part of the Good News. For instance, when he was speaking to the Ephesians he said, "Therefore having overlooked the times of ignorance, God is now declaring to men that all people everywhere should repent" (Acts 17:30 NASB). And later when he spoke to King Agrippa, he said he had preached repentance to "those in Damascus, then to those in Jerusalem and in all Judea, and to the Gentiles also" (Acts 26:20). Clearly Paul preached repentance as well as faith, and to turn from one's sin was considered to be an integral part of the Good News.

In Acts 2:38 we see Peter concluding his sermon on the day of Pentecost by saying, "Repent and be baptized, every one of you, in the name of Jesus Christ for the forgiveness of your sins. And you will receive the gift of the Holy Spirit." Then in Acts 3:19 in his second sermon Peter said, "Repent, then, and turn to God, so that your sins may be wiped out, that times of refreshing may come from the Lord." And finally in Acts 5:31, Peter said, "God exalted him to his own right hand as Prince and Savior that he might give repentance and forgiveness of sins to Israel."

Clearly the apostolic witness was careful to include the key element of repentance. In the nineteenth century General William Booth, the indomitable founder of the Salvation Army, prophesied that one of the chief dangers of the twentieth century would be a Christianity that lacked a focus on repentance. Sadly, his prophecy came true. And it is just as true for the twenty-first century.

Perhaps we have left repentance out of our witness because we don't hear teaching on it from the pulpit. Unfortunately, it is all too common to hear preaching that ignores repentance. The result is a reduced message that often sounds like this: "Just come tonight and make the decision to follow Jesus; get up out of your seats and come down the aisle and say 'yes' to him." I call it "reduced" because while it does call for trust to be placed in Jesus, the message neglects the call to turn from sin. This too easily leads to a name-only Christianity where there is profession of faith but no life transformation. People looking at the faith from the outside conclude that there is no difference between believer and unbeliever.

We may also avoid talking about repentance because the thought of calling friends and neighbours to turn from sin seems like a negative message. It is a hard message to deliver because people in our culture want to hear positive, soothing, and encouraging words. It costs us as preachers to deliver what appears to be a firm or harsh message. And some at least solve the problem by ignoring this part of the gospel. Tragically this indicates that we do not understand that repentance is a large part of the Good News.

When Paul and Silas shared the gospel with the largely pagan culture of Lystra they had no problem saying, "We are bringing you good news, telling you to turn from these worthless things to the living God" (Acts 14:15). For them telling people to turn from "worthless things" was part of the Good News. J. Edwin Orr, well-known writer and apologist, once said to me, "The first word of the gospel is repentance."

WITNESSING ABOUT THE TRUTH OF THE LAST JUDGMENT

Paul's experience and message in Acts 17 establish an excellent model for us as we consider the content of our witness. Paul was speaking largely to a secular or pagan culture with attitudes like those we are faced with today. Paul began his teaching with the good news of the resurrection (Acts 17:18) and near the end called for repentance, warned of the coming judgment, and finalized his teaching with another reminder of the resurrection. For Paul the Good News included both positive aspects like the resurrection and negative aspects like repentance and the coming judgment.

Many of us Christians must adjust our thinking. We need to understand that truths like repentance and the coming judgment are just as much a part of the overall Good News as is the substitutionary atonement and the resurrection. Perhaps if we were more careful to faithfully witness by giving out the whole truth, which includes repentance and the reality of judgment, we might see more success, both long term and short term.

I have observed that people are interested and open to the idea of judgment. On one occasion when ordering a coffee I simply asked the cashier how she was doing. Surprisingly she responded in a testy manner, saying, "Well, how do you expect I feel with the horrible news of all those children being murdered in Beslan?" She was referring to the aftermath of a recent terrorist attack in which hundreds of children were taken hostage, and the terrorists had killed many of them when the authorities mounted a rescue attempt. Her anguish was palpable.

I only had a few seconds, as there were people behind me waiting to order, but I said, "I feel the same pain, but the one thing that gives me some relief is this: I know that one day Christ will return, and the evil men who have committed such heinous murders will assuredly be judged." I still remember her stunned look.

Interestingly enough, one of the nearby cashiers who heard my comment said, "I agree with you."

Ray Comfort tells the following story, which illustrates how important it may be to recapture the scriptural model of witnessing about the coming judgment.

Two men are seated in a plane. The first is given a parachute and told to put it on because it will improve his flight. He is a little sceptical at first; he cannot see how wearing a parachute on board a plane could possibly improve his flight.

After some time, he decides to experiment and see if the claims are true. As he straps the apparatus to his back, he notices the weight of it on his shoulders and he finds he now has difficulty sitting upright. However, he consoles himself with the flight attendant's promise that the parachute will improve his flight, and he decides to give it a little time.

As the flight progresses, he notices that some of the other passengers are laughing at him because he is wearing a parachute inside the plane. He begins to feel somewhat humiliated. As they continue to laugh and point at him, he can stand it no longer. He sinks in his seat, unstraps the parachute, and throws it to the floor. Disillusionment and bitterness fills his heart because as far as he is concerned, he was told an outright lie.

The second man is also given a parachute, *but listen to what he is told*. He is told to put it on because at any moment he will have to jump out of the plane at 25,000 feet. He gratefully puts the parachute on. He does not notice the weight of it upon his shoulders, nor is he concerned that he cannot sit upright. His mind is consumed with the thought of what would happen to him if he jumped without the parachute.

Let's now analyze the motive and the result of each passenger's experience. The first man's motive for putting on the parachute was solely to improve his flight. The result of his experience was that he was humiliated by the other passengers, disillusioned, and somewhat embittered against those who gave him the parachute. As far as he is concerned, it will be a long time before anyone gets one of those things on his back again.

The second man put on the parachute solely to survive the jump to come. And because of his knowledge of what would happen to him if he jumped without it, he has a deep-rooted joy and peace in his heart, knowing that he has been saved from certain death. This knowledge gives him the ability to withstand the mockery of the other passengers. His attitude toward those who gave him the parachute is one of heartfelt gratitude...

Instead of preaching that Jesus will "improve the flight," we should be warning sinners that one day they will have to jump out of the plane. "It is appointed for men to die once, but after this the judgment" (Hebrews 9:27).[1]

QUESTIONS FOR GROUP DISCUSSION

1. Many religions offer a scheme or plan to show how we can find favour with God. Christianity also does this but from the outset emphasizes the actual person of Jesus. How should this be reflected in the way we carry out witnessing?

2. How prominent a place should the substitutionary atonement be given in our witnessing conversations? Can we expect this teaching to be gratefully received by people who do not see themselves as sinful?

3. The truth of the resurrection of Jesus from the dead is a strong focus of the New Testament. Since many in our day find it difficult to accept, should we make it a key focus of our teaching and speaking or not?

4. Was the teaching of repentance a key feature of apostolic preaching and teaching? And if so, should it also in our age be one of our key emphases as we speak to people about what it means to follow Jesus?

CHAPTER 6

Why It's Important to Know the Gospel

"The holiest life doesn't explain how to receive eternal
life. The Bible emphasizes our witness not apart from
words, but accompanied by words."
(R. Larry Moyer)

Christians universally agree that people must hear the
gospel before they can act on the message and respond
to it. I think, however, that many of us have never
given much thought to how we should prepare so we can be
witnesses. If we are going to share the Good News, we must
know how to explain it well. Therefore it is crucial for us to take
some training so we are prepared to share it with friends and
neighbours.

I have encountered people who think learning any kind of
a gospel presentation is bound to result in a "canned" approach,
lacking spontaneity. But that is not necessarily the case. We

would never apply this line of reasoning to a pastor and his work of preparing messages. Most of us would conclude that a minister who refused to diligently develop his sermons because he wanted to be spontaneous would not likely be of much help to his congregation.

The Bible calls us to "be ready to give a defense to everyone who asks you a reason for the hope that is in you" (1 Peter 3:15 NKJV). God is simply laying it out that we should be an equipped people, ready for the amazing work of sharing the Good News of Christ.

Ignorance is not bliss and in the case of witnessing can cause a negative outcome. This happened in a dramatic way at a church I was part of some years back. A fervent teenage Christian girl without knowledge of the basics of witnessing tried to share the gospel in a public place. Without warning she apparently began to act strangely. She started shouting at the people that they were wicked, evil, lost, and going to hell. While she had zeal and even compassion, she obviously lacked understanding about people, as evidenced by her clumsy and insensitive way of sharing the Good News. Perhaps the girl was taught to have compassion for lost people but given no training on how to share. This girl's sad experience is, to be sure, a rarity. I suspect the far more common outcome of lack of training for the average Christian is simply to opt for silence in the presence of unbelievers.

A friend of mine, Pastor Chris Timm, came to Christ in spite of a Christian's misplaced sensitivity. Through the particularly difficult and grievous experience of losing a child, Chris and his wife were inexplicably ministered to by a "presence" they both felt to be with them. They were not believers and did not know about the Holy Spirit. The only thing they knew for certain was that someone or something was with them who buoyed up their spirit and gave them comfort.

Convinced now there was a God, they began to seek him. Chris sought out a Christian friend, told him the story, and asked him about God. The friend was conflicted but in the end refrained from sharing truth because he didn't feel right about "intruding" on the grieving process.

The friend actually might have been capable of sharing the facts of the gospel with Chris, but in another sense he was not prepared, for he misread the heart cry of a fellow human being asking about God. I am convinced that if the friend had received training, even in the basics of sharing the gospel, he would have been able to help Chris find Christ sooner.

To be sure, examples like these two are rarities. Nevertheless, it appears that far too many Christians are simply unprepared to witness to their faith. This causes a scary and uncomfortable feeling and, worst of all, produces silent witnesses.

If we are called to perform an unfamiliar task and have no clue how to begin, most of us will not begin at all. Though we might want to, we are not likely to rise to the challenge. This is not a sign of weakness of character or something to be ashamed of but simply a sign that we need training.

Let us consider what average believers experience when they learn about their responsibility to witness. They often do not have a clear understanding themselves of the Good News. They already have a deep fear of deliberately going out to do something they think will probably result in failure, embarrassment, or both. A good many will end up with a vague sense of guilt, for they know they should be reaching out to people with the gospel. But most will choose to live with the guilt, since they have no concept of where to begin. To be ignorant of how to carry out a command of Scripture is to stand in a very uncomfortable place.

Contrast this with the fact that Jesus never sent out his disciples to share until they were trained. They had three and a half years of on-the-job experience with a master teacher. And even after that, they were told to wait until the Holy Spirit came to complete their preparation. It is simply not logical, nor does it fit the biblical model, that we should launch out to try to witness to people without receiving some kind of training.

Basic training should include mastering the content of the gospel, learning how to present this material, and mastering some basic people skills. A number of widely known presentations of the gospel are available; Evangelism Explosion, the bridge illustration, and the Romans Road presentation all have value. The particular presentation does not matter nearly so much as learning at least one and mastering it so well that at the drop of a hat in any circumstance you can confidently share it. Appendix 3 outlines a number of resources for training and direct evangelism purposes.

WITNESSING INVOLVES SHARING CONTENT

At some point witnessing to the Good News will include sharing basic content about Jesus Christ and the mission for which he came. We see this demonstrated in the book of Acts on numerous occasions when the apostles laid out the facts of who Jesus was, explained his death and what it meant, and preached the resurrection (Acts 2:22–41, 3:11–26, 4:8–12, 10:34–48). The Good News of Christ's life, death, resurrection, and ascension is simple historical fact. It contains specific content that we can and must impart to others.

Witnessing can also include the sharing of our experience of Jesus. The reality that we have put faith and trust in Christ, that we now follow him, and that we have an ongoing relationship with him are also facts to be shared. Paul used personal testimony powerfully on three occasions recorded in the book of Acts (9:2; 22:6–16;26:12). He spoke in detail of his experience of coming to Christ. I believe God had these testimonies included in Scripture to teach us that what we have personally experienced with Christ is important and should be passed on.

Note that we do not have to impart a lot of content each time we share. In fact, in a particular incident of sharing we may have only a brief opportunity to speak a few words that fit the situation. For example, one afternoon I witnessed to a doorman on my way to a doctor's appointment and half an hour later to my doctor by casually sharing that I was a Christ-follower. There was no time or opportunity to fully share who Christ is and what he did, but there was an opening to confess his name. Incidentally, the doorman was quite delighted to hear that I was a Christian and confessed himself to also be a follower of Christ.

On other occasions, I have shared in depth about Christ and the way of receiving the gift of salvation. To do that properly I had to have a good grasp of biblical truth. It was also crucial to have a plan or structure to share this Good News. I have acquired both through training and practice.

BENEFITS OF BEING PREPARED TO SHARE

I first learned the importance of being well prepared to witness through Professor Murray Downey, who taught evangelism at our Bible college. When I first met him he was already white-haired and a little stooped, and he appeared to have one foot across the threshold of retirement. However, he was fervent for God, clear-headed, and deadly serious about imparting to us students a method of sharing the Good News. The most memorable part of the course was a weekend of evangelism and outreach near the end of the year when the class witnessed in a small rural town near Regina, Saskatchewan. A few of us took turns street-preaching, using a hand-held megaphone, while the rest went house to house until we had virtually covered the little town. We were confidently sharing the Good News because Professor Downey had taught the entire class a simple way of sharing the gospel.

Over the three months of class instruction and one-on-one training, virtually the whole class had learned the basics of sharing a specific presentation of the Good News of Christ. Because of that coaching, we had not only specific content to share but also a measure of confidence and boldness to do so. Years later in a class I taught to Bible students in Mexico I followed the same pattern, including the witnessing weekend, with the same results. As students went door to door in a small village they knowledgeably and confidently shared Christ.

Training made a crucial difference to a woman named Rosa. When I first met her in the 1990s she was under significant stress and seemed to be highly emotional and needy. After a few years I left the church we both attended and lost touch with her. When we met again through a chance encounter I accepted her invitation to visit a new church plant where she had been involved for about six months. There I discovered that Rosa was one of the key people involved in door-to-door evangelism.

I was astonished. She was one of the last people I would have expected to be involved in this kind of ministry. She told me about various changes in her life that had helped her to move into this new ministry. But perhaps the most important was this: she had taken training in evangelism.

It would be a mistake to conclude that being prepared and feeling competent to share the gospel is the whole story in witnessing. It is not. But it is also a mistake to minimize its importance. We must not overlook the fact that Jesus took time to train his disciples to be witnesses. Indeed, it occupied much of the scarce time he had to spend in his earthly ministry.

Learning content is only one aspect of preparing to witness. Another is learning how to bridge the empty spaces that exist between people, almost like buffer zones. In the next section, we'll learn how to build bridges so that we truly connect with those whom Christ has called us to love.

QUESTIONS FOR GROUP DISCUSSION

1. Most of us would agree that zeal to obey Christ in the matter of sharing is very important. But how important do you think it is that training be imparted to the person who has a desire to witness?

2. We would all agree that it is much easier to simply tell someone to do something than to show them. Is this one of the reasons why the church finds it difficult to train people in witnessing and evangelism?

3. I told the story of a Christian who did not offer a witness to a grieving seeker. What may have been other factors in the decision of this Christian not to share Christ with his grieving friend?

4. We often characterize the disciples as being untrained fishermen. But how might it be instructive for us to see that they actually received quite extensive training by Jesus himself for their mission of witness and evangelism?

5. Does witnessing only "count" if we get to share the whole substitutionary atonement? Or can we share Christ even in brief conversations?

6. Is it important to learn a presentation of the gospel, or is it better to simply be spontaneous and speak as we are led by the Spirit?

CHAPTER 7

Building Bridges

"We must not become undercover Christians or rabbit-hole Christians. Rabbit-hole Christians pop their heads out only when they must…They live with the unspoken motto, the less contact with non-Christians the better the day. They pop out to get in the car to run their Christian kids to the Christian school. They listen to their Christian radio station, run off to their Christian Bible study, then go to lunch with their Christian friend…When that is a description of our lives, Jesus is not impressed."
(Dave Early)

In our pluralistic Canada we often bump into people who seem to inhabit a different world from us. At a local store here in Guelph, Ontario, I often see middle-aged women with their younger daughters in tow, garbed in long, shapeless, nondescript blue or green patterned dresses. The mother sports a grim black hat-like covering that tightly clings to her head. It is always a little shocking to bump into these Amish folk—like encountering something strange in the midst of the familiar. But they are of course no stranger than the women who walk our streets garbed in long black robes with head coverings and sometimes face coverings that hide everything except their eyes.

We live in a country of many subcultures and could easily let the minor and major culture differences in lifestyles produce a chasm between us. It is possible on any given day to encounter Sikhs, Hindus, Muslims, Amish people, heavily tattooed bikers, flocks of young people, people on the liberal-left spectrum, people on the conservative-right spectrum, Hispanics, African-Canadians, Chinese, gays and lesbians, and perhaps a few Christians.

Bridge building is crucial for all of us who want to speak with our families, neighbours, friends, and acquaintances. In some cases it means creating connections when the culture differences and worldviews that separate us are obvious, like our clothing or differing religious worldviews. In other cases, though we may largely share the same cultural heritage, we have to bridge radically different worldviews. To find a way to connect with neighbours and those who may become friends we must seek to build bridges of friendship and commonality. This chapter will explore how to build these bridges so we can walk across them to connect with people whom Jesus has called us to love and reach.

Building Bridges by Acceptance, Not Condemnation

One of the major ways in which many of us need to change is to become people who radically accept others. We Christians tend to be uptight about people engaging in sin. Now somebody may be asking, "So what's your point? Aren't we supposed to condemn sin?" Well, my point is that our uptightness tends to make us into a people who exude judgment. We are often unaware that our body language sends out the message that we are uncomfortable around sinners. I suspect that all too often they perceive us as judgmental.

All sorts of behaviours bother us. For instance, we don't know how to hide our discomfort around people who swear. In an Internet video clip published by City News, Canadians were described as being more foulmouthed than their British or US counterparts.[1] Recently while I was in a Tim Hortons coffee shop one of the patrons enjoying an early morning coffee with his friends let loose with a vulgar profanity. My spirit automatically recoiled even as my mind was reasoning, "That is typical behaviour for a 'normal' Canadian, and I must not be overly shocked."

Alex, a young Christian friend of mine, is an example of someone who manages his reactions well. Within a few days of him starting a new job, the other employees surmised something was different about him. After a time, they began to apologize for their foul language when he was in earshot. He had not said anything about his own beliefs or condemned their language but had simply walked the talk—his way of speaking without cursing caused him to stand out from his colleagues.

I had a different and less happy experience many years ago, when I asked a profane co-worker if he would clean up his language when he was around me. I spoke to him privately and respectfully, but the few times we met later on he acted disdainfully towards me. Clearly, he had been offended. I think I had pushed him away.

Many evangelicals to this day view drinking as sinful and find being around drunken people problematic. I could go on and on, but the basic issue is that our uptightness with people's "sinful" behaviour provokes us to not want to be around them. How unfortunate, because we somehow transmit our discomfort, and the people we are seeking to reach sense that we would rather not be with them.

This issue is far bigger than most evangelicals realize. Consciously or subconsciously most of us walk around with a sin-o-meter running. It is all well and good to say, "Love the sinner, hate the sin," but many of us are a lot better at communicating disgust or even hatred for sin (and maybe the sinner too) than we are at communicating love and acceptance.

Many Christians feel ill at ease in the company of people who have embraced homosexuality or those who may be cohabiting without benefit of marriage. Don't get me wrong here. There will certainly come a time to speak about sin. But just maybe that conversation should take place further along in the relationship.

It is instructive to see that Jesus went to the house of Zacchaeus, a notorious sinner, to have a meal (Luke 19), and only later did Zacchaeus repent of sin. Similarly, Jesus reached out first in love and acceptance to the Samaritan woman and only later brought out the sin in her life (John 4). Somehow we must do better at communicating deep love and acceptance to imperfect people. Jesus did it. Perhaps that's why the common people loved to be around him.

I was once at an outdoor barbecue with some Mexican friends where a lot of young children were playing around, acting up, and occasionally getting into trouble. An older and very wise Mexican friend captured our attention by saying, "Why just look at those children getting into all that trouble and making all that mess! Can you believe it? You know what I think? I think they're acting…just like children." His point of course was that adults should expect children to get into trouble and messes, for that is part of their nature as children. And, likewise, when we see people in the world who are yet outside of Christ acting like they are not Christians, perhaps we should be less surprised and a lot more gracious and loving, since they are simply doing what comes naturally.

LET'S BUILD BRIDGES BY LOVING SO THAT WE CAN LOVE MORE
As Christians who long to share the Good News of Christ with others we may be accused of loving those around us with an ulterior motive. For example, many of us see love and compassion as the necessary first step in building a relationship. But some say that our true motive is to send a packet of gospel information over the relationship bridge that has been built by love. And they would see us as being manipulative because we have an ulterior motive behind our action of reaching out in love.

Now we need to confront this accusation head on. Is it wrong to love people if we have another long-range motive in mind? Personally, I do not believe there is any ethical problem here. We need to see that loving people in the present moment should indeed cause a relationship bridge to form. And this relationship will then make a way to love these same people even more, because we will be in a new position that allows us to share the gospel with them.

Since we believe that the gospel is the most wonderful message ever given and will bring the greatest possible blessing to those who receive it, to *not* speak this Good News to people would be to withhold love from needy people. There is nothing wrong with loving people with an ulterior motive as long as that motive is not manipulative. To love in the present so that more love can be expressed in the future is surely a good thing! The problem arises when we harbour a project mentality that loves people *only* because they are viewed as potential receivers of the Good News we want to share.

I read some time ago an example of how this can go very wrong. It concerns an atheist who at the present time is pushing his agenda for euthanasia. When he was in high school some Christian friends shared truth with him and invited him to become a Christian. Imagine his shock and hurt when upon his rejection of the gospel his friends dropped him. From his perspective he was loved and appreciated not for himself but as a kind of a project by these Christian "friends," who in the end turned out to be no friends at all.

I believe there is an even better way. Jesus calls us clearly in Matthew 22:37–40 to love God first and secondly to "Love your neighbor as yourself." We should never cease to love people even if they say "No" to Jesus. People are not projects; they are precious human beings who are to be loved and cherished for who they are.

Several winters ago we had heavy snowfalls where we live in Ontario. One day when Linda, my wife, and I were shovelling our driveway she noticed a nearby neighbour doing the same. Quickly she whispered to me, "Let's go and help her; her husband's sick, and she's on her own." So away we went. We started to get to know her, and after helping with shovelling a few more times that winter we began to have a relationship with both husband and wife.

Several months later we started a Bible study in our home, hoping that some of our neighbours would come. We weren't particularly close to the neighbours we had helped, so it was a surprise when they came for the ten- week study. We found out that they had family members who were Christian, and they had been wanting to know more about Christianity for some time. Who knew? God did—so he sent someone to build a bridge.

LET'S BUILD BRIDGES TO CASUAL ACQUAINTANCES

Almost every day we have opportunities to witness to people we know in a casual kind of way. For instance, we cross paths with the same cashiers in grocery stores, the same tellers in banks, and the same vendors at the farmers' market. On these occasions we rarely have time or opportunity to speak the whole truth, but we do have time to work on building bridges of love and acceptance. A smile, using someone's name, being interested in others and open about ourselves are just a few of the ways we can make these connections significant ones.

The Explosive Power of a Smile

One day while riding my bicycle I saw a man walking the pathway coming in my direction. I was going slowly at that point, and I briefly smiled at him as I passed by. About seven kilometres later on my way home I met the same man in a parking lot, greeted him, and stopped to chat. We exchanged business cards and later on met for coffee.

He then told me something that grabbed my attention. He said, "You know, when our paths first crossed and you smiled at me as you passed by on your bike, I knew you were an okay guy." A passing smile to a complete stranger was all it took. That smile became the bridge that later led to Christ being confessed before men.

My wife never tires of telling the story of a smile that changed her life when she was a university student. She was not yet a Christian, and in the midst of troubling circumstances she found herself depressed and totally without hope for the future. But in her daily walk about the campus she repeatedly passed a young woman who always smiled at her. My wife didn't know her, but Linda was struck by the thought that even if she, personally, didn't have any reason to smile, there must yet be some hope in the world.

About a year later, after Linda had become a follower of Christ, she met this same "smiling person" at a Christian conference. That friendly smile was like a light shining in darkness, and God used it in Linda's life to keep her going forward to that moment when she was able to hear the Good News and receive it.

The Revolutionary Power of Calling People by Name

In our ordinary day-to-day lives we repeatedly have contact with service people wearing name tags. Bank tellers, store cashiers, and Tim Hortons attendants wear them as part of their uniform. I make it a practise to greet these people casually by name as they are serving me. It almost always elicits a pleasant response, because it gives them the sense that they are being treated as people rather than robots or menial labourers. Sometimes the name is so unusual that it leads to further conversations.

To be sure, some people do not respond, but over the years it has been clear that the vast majority of people sincerely appreciate being treated as fellow humans. It has also been in some cases the beginning of a relationship that otherwise might never have been born.

The Astonishing Power of Demonstrating Interest in People

I was taking a walk in the late afternoon on a beautifully kept walking path in a major Canadian city when a man walked past me. He was driving his walking stick forcefully into the path ahead of him as he took each step. I seized the opportunity to ask him about this unusual form of walking. When he graciously responded I noted that he spoke with an accent. I then asked him about the accent, and he said that he was from Iraq.

I had never met anyone from Iraq before and told him how delighted I was to meet him. Then I asked if that meant he was a Muslim. He somewhat defensively admitted that he was. I then told him how pleased I was to meet him, because back in my home city I had recently met a number of Muslims and had been asking questions about their faith. I went on to ask him if I might ask him a few questions about Islam.

For the next hour while we walked together on that beautiful path my new friend, Aladdin, and I talked about Islam. But we also talked about Christianity and Jesus, for in the give and take of conversation I had an amazing opportunity to fully share the core beliefs of my own faith. When it was time to part, both of us were loath to end the conversation. Indeed, he asked if I might meet him the next day to continue our chat. Unfortunately, I could not, as I was leaving the city early the next morning. Upon hearing that, and knowing we probably would not meet again, he shook my hand most warmly, looked me directly in the eye, and told me with intense emotion in his voice, "You must keep on doing what you are doing."

The Remarkable Power Released by Being Transparent

I think that Christians are often hesitant to confess to strangers that they are followers of Christ. Probably most of us consider it safer to not volunteer too much information about ourselves. It is noteworthy that in a passage where the context is about overcoming fear, Christ said, "Whoever acknowledges me before men, I will also acknowledge him before my Father in heaven" (Matthew 10:32).

Some time ago I returned a package of stale cookies to a local grocery store. The cashier serving me was apologetic, indicating several times how sorry she was. I looked her straight in the eyes and said, "Hey, it's okay; you're forgiven…I'm a follower of Christ, and that's what he calls me to do." Her head literally snapped back in astonishment.

A friend of mine, Brenda, recently moved to our city. Her great desire is to always be on mission for Christ, but that day she was so preoccupied and harried with the details of moving that she did not think she was in a position to witness. But a surprising encounter took place in a local coffee shop. Brenda confided to the cashier that she and her husband were brand new to Guelph, having moved that same day. When asked what brought them to Guelph, my friend replied, "We came because we've always loved this city, but we're also excited to be involved in starting a new church." The cashier was very interested, asked more questions, and positively responded to an invitation to come to church.

On another occasion, I thought the person attending me in a store looked familiar. So I said, "I wonder where we may have met before."

Finally we decided that we didn't know each other, but Al (not his real name) said, "Maybe we knew each other in a former life."

"I don't think so," I said. A short while later I volunteered that I was a follower of Christ and I believed the biblical view that we have only one life. In fact I quoted the verse, "Just as man is destined to die once, and after that to face judgment" (Hebrews 9:27).

Al was open to further conversation, and I mentioned that I had recently written an article on reincarnation. We parted amicably, but I returned the next day with a copy of that article, which he gladly received. In this case, a short discussion about spiritual things opened the door to giving someone a piece of literature that presented the gospel in some detail. Our willingness to be transparent about our faith will often open doors that otherwise would have stayed shut.

Of course, openly confessing that we follow Christ is not the whole gospel. However, we have at the very least spoken the name of Jesus and planted a seed in people's minds and hearts that just maybe there's something to this Christianity after all. Jesus himself certainly taught his followers to be open before men when he said in Matthew 10:32–33, "Whoever acknowledges me before men, I will also acknowledge him before my Father in heaven. But whoever disowns me before men, I will disown him before my Father in heaven." Moreover, we never know where the conversation might lead once we open up about who we are.

I believe our willingness to simply be transparent about being followers of Christ honours Jesus. I also believe it has the potential to open many doors for deeper conversation with people whom God is calling into his light.

LET'S BUILD BRIDGES TO OUR "BURDEN-OF-CARE" PEOPLE

The world is filled with people, and we cannot possibly witness to them all. That is why we must pay special attention to a group of people I call our "burden-of-care" people. All of us have particular social networks of people we are relatively close to. There are family members, colleagues at work, friends in the Rotary association, and acquaintances at the gym or the badminton club with whom we already have an established relationship.

From a purely practical point of view it's logical to seek to deepen relationships within this pool of people. They know us already; it's not like we are starting from zero in forming a relationship. These people should be given a special priority in prayer and our making time to be with them. God has placed them in our world, and it would be a folly to ignore them. It's noteworthy that in Luke's Gospel when the formerly demon-possessed man wanted to follow Jesus, he was told instead to go home and tell his family what great things the Lord had done for him.

I regret that I blew an opportunity to build a bridge of friendship with my family when I came to faith in Christ. At eighteen years of age, I left my home in Saskatchewan and went to Brampton, Ontario, to seek my fortune. Along with my twin brother, Roger, I was boarding with an older brother and his wife. At that time I heard the Good News about Christ and made a personal commitment to follow him, and my life changed dramatically, especially how I spent my time. I was away at church all day Sunday and out two or three nights a week with church friends. My whole life revolved around the church. I had found not only Christ but a network of new friends and activities.

What I didn't see at the time was that I had virtually abandoned Roger and the rest of my family with whom I was living. I deeply lament that now. We need to be careful that we don't allow the power of our new passion for our faith to hurt relationships that God wants us to nurture.

William Turner tells the story of Pastor Palmer Ofuoku, a distinguished preacher in his native Nigeria. As a boy the young Ofuoku, though not from a Christian family, was sent to a Christian mission station to get an education. Some of the missionaries were distant and clearly felt themselves superior. Then a new missionary came to the school and began to develop close emotional relationships with some of the Nigerians, including young Palmer. Eventually Palmer came to faith in Christ. Although he was not equally impressed with all the missionaries, he later said of this particular worker, "He built a bridge of friendship to me, and Jesus walked across."[2]

We should regularly pray for family, friends, colleagues, and acquaintances and regularly seek to be with them, deepening the friendships, loving them as we can. Then, sooner or later, we can expect God to give us opportunities to witness openly and naturally into their lives with words as well as actions.

The building of bridges is important work and one we don't do alone. In many instances other people have already had a hand in building connections to those we witness to. When the seed of the Good News is sown, even in the smallest kind of way, we never know just how God may use it. We are simply to do our part to deliberately sow the seed in as many ways as possible to as many people as possible.

QUESTIONS FOR GROUP DISCUSSION

1. Are Christians so immersed in our own subculture and worldview that we have effectively cut ourselves off from the wider culture? How can we begin to build bridges out of our isolation?

2. Is it common for unbelievers to feel judged and condemned when they are around you? Do you have a type of sin-o-metre running at all times? How might you begin to live so that people are not uptight around you?

3. Is there a danger that in building bridges to people we will simply see them as projects? How can we guard our own hearts so that we will avoid this trap?

4. To what extent do our own imperfections and sins keep us from being transparent about Christ in our lives?

5. Being transparent with people about our own lives is hugely important. Why then do we find it hard to do this? What is it that causes us to "hide" from people?

6. What does the author mean by "burden-of-care people"? Are these people easier or harder to talk to than an acquaintance whom we have just met?

CHAPTER 8

Seed Sowing: More Important Than We Think

"Success is sharing your faith and living your life for Jesus Christ. It has nothing whatsoever to do with bringing anyone to the Lord. It has everything to do with obedience." (Bill Fay)

Remember this: Whoever sows sparingly will also reap sparingly, and whoever sows generously will also reap generously (2 Corinthians 9:6).

One of Jesus' most memorable parables was all about sowing seeds:

That same day Jesus went out of the house and sat by the lake. Such large crowds gathered around him that he got into a boat and sat in it, while all the people stood on the shore. Then he told them many things in parables, saying:

"A farmer went out to sow his seed. As he was scattering the seed, some fell along the path, and the birds came and ate it up. Some fell on rocky places, where it did not have much soil. It sprang up quickly, because the soil was shallow. But when the sun came up, the plants were scorched, and they withered because they had no root. Other seed fell among thorns, which grew up and choked the plants. Still other seed fell on good soil, where it produced a crop—a hundred, sixty or thirty times what was sown. He who has ears, let him hear" (Matthew 13:1–9).

SOULS TAKE TIME TO GERMINATE

In many cases when we witness we will sow the seed of the Good News about Jesus and not see immediate results. However, this should not trouble us. Rightly understood, "seed planting" as a metaphor for witness leads us to expect a natural time lag between the sowing of gospel seed and the harvest of conversion. Many of us, however, have been trained to anticipate immediate results from our witnessing activity, which sets us up for frustration and a sense of failure.

The final results of witnessing and evangelism can be a long time in coming. In my own case, from the initial planting of seed to conversion took about fifteen years. Some occasions of seed planting were in-depth conversations, while others involved only a few words. In some cases, Christians demonstrated love and compassion, godly acts that spoke silently but powerfully.

When I was five or six, my three siblings and I slept in a large open room that was often dark and somewhat scary. One night, in the inky blackness my elder brother taught us the Lord's prayer (maybe because he was scared himself). I memorized it, and it started my young mind thinking about God. A seed was sown.

When I was older some people came to our school and told us about a free summer Bible camp they were running in our area. Mom and Dad were fine with us going, which was not surprising since we didn't have a lot of money. At that camp I clearly heard the gospel (I can still remember the first sermon I ever heard). I went home with a new Bible as a gift and carefully put it away where it wouldn't get lost. Occasionally I pulled it out of the drawer and tried to make sense of it.

In my late teens, just after I finished high school, I began dating a committed Christian girl from a local evangelical church. We often spoke of spiritual things; in fact, that's almost all we talked about. I learned years later to my chagrin that she wasn't dating me for my captivating personality but rather because she saw an opportunity to witness to me.

Dan, another high school friend, was a sincere Christian who often witnessed to me and lived a godly life before me. He invited me to church and on occasion would share the gospel with me by inviting me to listen to taped messages with him.

All through my high school years I listened regularly to a radio preacher who mostly focused on prophecy and the end times. His content was so riveting that I enrolled in a Bible correspondence course and started to learn the basics of the Bible. Through this course I memorized a verse of Scripture that God would later use at a point of crisis to bring me to himself.

In my late teens, when I was far from home and going through a tough time, I received a letter from my sister, Lucy, who was particularly close to me. In that letter she transparently shared how God had recently helped her through a trying time. It was a simple word, but I was much impacted, and not long after I repented from my sins and put my faith in Christ as Saviour and Lord.

Paul refers to the act of sowing in evangelism and expands the metaphor by including the act of watering:

What, after all, is Apollos? And what is Paul? Only servants, through whom you came to believe—as the Lord has assigned to each his task. I planted the seed, Apollos watered it, but God made it grow. So neither he who plants nor he who waters is anything, but only God, who makes things grow. The man who plants and the man who waters have one purpose, and each will be rewarded according to his own labour. For we are God's fellow workers; you are God's field, God's building (1 Corinthians 3:5–9).

Here the Bible makes it clear that a process of time is involved in a person coming to Christ. Furthermore, a number of people are involved in the process: someone sows the seed, and others are expected to water it. And finally, lest anyone should become proud, Paul is definite that God himself causes the seed to grow—or to put it another way, it is God who causes the person who has heard the gospel to ultimately believe and embrace it.

We Should Sow as Widely as Possible

Since harvest and conversion cannot happen without the seed of the gospel being sown, Christians should intentionally pursue sowing as widely as they possibly can. If a farmer desires to harvest a large crop, you can be sure he will sow as much seed in as many fields as he can. The same principle is true of witnessing.

Even though the context of 2 Corinthians 9:6 is all about giving, it holds true for witnessing as well. In other words, "Those who sow sparingly will reap sparingly." We must witness widely if we expect to someday reap a large harvest.

Jesus certainly had this burden. In Mark 1, the disciples found him in a solitary place where he had gone to pray and told him that everyone was looking for him. Jesus simply said, "Let us go somewhere else—to the nearby villages—so I can preach there also. That is why I have come" (Mark 1:38). Since we are "sent ones," even as Jesus was sent by the Father, we should model ourselves after him by also sowing the gospel widely.

Since sowing widely is such a worthy goal, we must ask ourselves how we must live so that it will occur in our lives. If at present we seem to have few or no opportunities to witness, it seems logical to ask ourselves how we might begin to live differently so we have more openings.

Our first step is to meet and get to know new people. If we do not make new contacts, we are condemning ourselves to sowing over and over in ground that has already received seed. So how then do we meet new people?

We can intentionally put ourselves in situations where we have the opportunity to get to know non-believers. This sounds simple but may require a radical shift in our thinking. Most believers largely orient their lives around other Christians. In addition to being at church services we have church committees to work on, prayer groups to commit to, various teaching and discipleship programs to join, as well as legitimate social connections to maintain that usually involve other believers. At the end of the day we have virtually zero time or energy left in our busy lives. As a result we have little room to meet or get to know non-believers. To break out of this mindset and practice will demand a firm intentionality.

Serving people outside the church is one avenue to consider. For instance, most neighbourhoods have volunteer groups looking for an extra set of helping hands. School committees, neighbourhood associations, and even security patrols organized by the police are places where we can volunteer.

Serving people through a church ministry is also effective. One church runs a coffeehouse at the front of its sanctuary during the week where volunteers serve guests who come for coffee and a doughnut. Another church I know of puts on a supper for street people twice a week and is always looking for volunteers.

Volunteering will put us in close contact with fellow volunteers who may not be Christians as well as with the clients we serve. No, our mere presence is not enough for witness, but it is the starting place for witnessing to occur. Only by actually spending time with non-Christians, as Christ did when he lived among us, can we ever hope to have some kind of seed-sowing witness among them.

We could join social clubs and learn to square dance or line dance or even take up ballroom dancing. We could join a local gym and during our workout times begin to get to know some hard-core pressers of iron. Those interested in sports could join a club for tennis, volleyball, racquetball, badminton, darts, pickle ball, biking, or even billiards.

Small things can offer significant starting points. What about making a goal to learn and remember the names of people that you do business with in your neighbourhood? Most of us go to the same grocery stores, banks, and corner stores, where we see the same people. If we took the trouble to learn their names instead of treating them as mere functionaries, we would have a pool of people with whom a relationship would be possible. While we will not go on to have close ties with all of them, we will almost certainly, by the providence of God, have some new relationships and in due course have opportunities to share.

This was vividly demonstrated to me when I recently went to get a haircut. I usually go to the same place so I can get to know the staff. The shop was virtually empty except for Jocelyn (not her real name), who had cut my hair six months earlier. I didn't remember much of our former conversation, but it didn't matter, because she was lonely, bored, and semi-depressed. She was also amazed that I had come into the shop just at her moment of need.

Jocelyn remembered that I was a pastor and immediately wanted to talk about spiritual things. The entire time she spent cutting my hair was passed in spiritual conversation. When it was time to pay the bill, I sensed that she didn't really want me to leave. So I asked if she would like me to pray for her. She said, "Oh, would you be willing to do that?" So I did.

As I prayed I continued to witness to truth, praying that her sins might be forgiven in Jesus. When I finished she wondered if I had been reading her mind, for my words had expressed the will of her heart.

This story points out that a "small" witness six months previously of merely confessing Christ, in the end, was not small at all. Rather, it was a significant first step, which led to a much fuller witness to the truth of Jesus six months later.

Sharing hobbies and interests is another great way of meeting new people. A friend of mine belongs to a club where members meet regularly to share war stories about their unique hobby—collecting fountain pens. He tells me that he has had some significant opportunities to witness. A woman in Southern Ontario who likes to read used that love of reading to make a bridge to others. She planned, promoted, and organized a reading club that meets in her home every six weeks or so. This has provided numerous opportunities to share Christ with women in the neighbourhood.

Two of my hobbies are weight training and bicycling. I could just stay at home and lift weights, but instead I joined a local gym for the express purpose of meeting new people. One of my neighbours likes to go bike riding with me, and on several occasions our conversation has been focused on Christian truth almost from the beginning to the end of our ride. I plan on inviting other neighbours to join me on the bike trails, and I look for God to open doors so that I might bear witness to this Christ who has sent me out on mission.

Some Christians avoid witnessing because meeting new people makes them uncomfortable. Some think that witnessing is only for extroverts. However, God calls both extroverts and introverts and all the shades between to answer the call to witness.

QUESTIONS FOR GROUP DISCUSSION

1. What do we mean when we speak of witnessing as "sowing the seed"? How might this be different from a full-orbed presentation of the gospel?

2. How can the concept of "sowing gospel seed" help us to be less uptight in our attempts to witness to people?

3. Count up how many people sowed "seed" into your life before you responded to Jesus. Then share that briefly with your group.

4. If we understand that sowing the "gospel seed" is largely imparting a piece of information, what might "watering" the seed consist of?

5. Is it logical to expect a large scale return from a planting of only a few seeds? Why not? What needs to happen so that a great harvest may be reaped?

6. Is it possible to plant the seed of the gospel widely if almost all of our friends and acquaintances are fellow believers?

What is the solution to this problem? Don't be afraid to be creative.

CHAPTER 9

How Can the Introverted Carry Out Their Witness?

"Being an extrovert isn't essential to evangelism… obedience and love are." (Rebecca Manley Pippert)

"Some people believe that evangelism is only reserved for "A" type personalities. Nothing could be further from the truth." (Dave Early and David Wheeler)

"I'm willing to bet the farm that in our post–modern Christian society the most important evangelistic skill is listening." (Todd Hunter)

B ooks on witnessing rarely, if ever, discuss how being an introvert influences how we share our faith. Extroverts sometimes do not see the importance of this issue at all; they simply wonder why the introvert doesn't "get over it" and start acting like them. Introverts seem to know instinctively that the distinction between these two personality types is crucial to our theme of witnessing.

An extroverted person may adopt with ease many of the suggestions and practices that the introvert would find almost impossible to act upon. We do a disservice to people if we do not acknowledge this fundamental difference between personalities. We shall see that introverts are just as much called to witness as are extroverts but are not under any obligation to carry out their mission in the same manner.

Generally, introverts are seen as somewhat shy and retiring, people who do not pursue relationships aggressively and often seem to be content when alone with their own thoughts, reading a book, or pursuing another solitary pastime. In his book *Introverts in the Church,* Adam McHugh adds a little more technical content to the description. He describes an introvert as:

1) A person who gets energy from being alone, as opposed to finding it in the company of others.
2) A person who processes information internally by thinking and mulling it over, as opposed to thinking out loud in the company of others while coming to a conclusion.
3) A person who prefers depth over breadth in most aspects of their life.[1]

Introverts often prefer to relax alone or with a few close friends and need rest after group activities, even ones they enjoy. They dislike small talk but can talk a lot about subjects that are important to them. They tend to think before they speak or act, have great powers of concentration, prefer to work on their own rather than in a group, may prefer written communication, and do not share private thoughts with many people.[2]

An estimated 60 to 70 percent of North Americans are introverted, but most methods of evangelism popular among Christians today lend themselves far more to extroverted people. Introverts in the church who are exposed to some of these ideas and methods may find themselves more depressed than helped to be effective witnesses.

I've heard extroverts tell "success" stories that utterly failed to inspire the majority of introverts present. Even worse, such stories often discourage them because they cannot see themselves doing something similar. The introverted person at times thinks, whether he says it or not, "Well, that's fine for you, because that's how God made you, but what about me?"

I suspect that some introverts have concluded that they are not called to bear witness since, in their eyes, they do not have the skill set necessary to talk to others. Many think that it takes glib talking, pushy manners, and an outgoing, gregarious personality to engage in witnessing. Since this is not who they are, they conclude that witnessing must not be for them. However, as Adam McHugh puts it, "Introverts do not receive an evangelism exemption."[3]

People with a more introverted bent might even wonder if God's plan is to change them into extroverts so they can do the job like some of the models that have been held up before them. However, God uses people of all personality types. For example, a good many of the numerous missionaries I've known have been introverted, rather than extroverted. Yet God chose to use them in effective witnessing.

Some Christians might object to our using terms like "shy" or "introvert" to describe ourselves. They believe that our personalities are renewed at conversion, and with the help of the Holy Spirit any and every Christian can and must bear witness. In a sense they are not wrong; Scripture confirms that the timid Timothy types as well as the assertive apostle Paul types are to fulfill the work of the ministry, including evangelism (2 Timothy 1:6–8, 4:5). Nevertheless God does give us different personalities from birth, and in Scripture we see him using different types of people in different ways.

One more thing: "introversion" and "shyness" are not synonyms. While areas overlap, one can be an introvert and yet not be shy. I am, for example, predominately an introvert yet am by no means shy and at times am even gregarious in relating to people. On the other hand I know other introverts who are fundamentally shy people as well. In their day-to-day experience, they do not go out of their way to meet new people. It simply is not natural for them.

So if we take it for granted that God calls people from all personality types into his kingdom, we can also take it for granted that God has ways to use all of those personality types for the building of his kingdom. It's time now to explore the particular roles and means that the introvert by temperament is naturally suited to fulfill.

Witnessing by Playing the Supportive Role

Introverts may avoid participating in witnessing programs like Christianity Explored, Alpha, or H2O because they usually have difficulty initiating spiritual conversations. But what if they were to become involved in team ministry with other Christians?

For example, when using witnessing programs the quiet and more reflective person does not have to be the upfront person leading the session. People are needed to work behind the scenes, helping in meal preparation, doing clean up, making reminder telephone calls, being part of the prayer team, and even picking up people who need a ride to the meeting.

Some years ago my wife, Linda, and I were assigned along with a small team of local people to plant a church in a suburb of Buenos Aires. The extroverts on that team led the worship and preached the sermons in our small home church. Over a few years the church grew. It rented its own facility and today has its own building. But it would never have seen the light of day if not for the background practical work of the quiet ones, who cleaned the house, prepared the food, and did all the practical things necessary so that people could be welcomed in to hear the Good News of Jesus. It seems very appropriate for extroverts and introverts to pool their respective personalities for the work of making the name of Jesus famous.

WITNESSING BY CULTIVATING DEEP RELATIONSHIPS

All Christians should be involved in deepening relationships with unbelievers, no matter where they score on the extrovert/introvert scale. The extroverted person finds it relatively easy to make new relationships, but since this is difficult for introverts they could focus more on increasing the depth of relationship with persons they already know.

My mother-in-law, Kay, was a master at doing this. Always in a spirit of prayer, over a period of years she deepened relationships with neighbours she already knew. As time passed some of these people came to Christ, and they joined Kay in the prayer group she had set up in her home. Some young people, friends of her daughters, actually came to live in her house for a while. In that setting much time was given to listening and to growing a much deeper relationship bridge. Eventually the Good News of Jesus passed over that bridge, and some of those people became followers of Jesus.

I do not want to leave the impression that introverts cannot form new links with new people, for they can. One of the easiest ways to accomplish this is to pursue a group interest such as a sport, a hobby, or anything in which people gather together for play or competition or a mutual interest of any kind. The interest itself is both a buffer for the introvert who finds relating somewhat difficult and a bridge to forming new relationships.

Witnessing by Intentionally Self-identifying as a Christian

In many Canadian cities you can and will encounter Muslims and Sikhs while walking down the street. These two groups self-identify to the onlooker, announcing their religious affiliation by the clothes they wear. They are not ashamed of their hijabs or their turbans.

By contrast the vast majority of Christians may be missing opportunities to self-identify and thereby confess Christ. Doing something to self-identify as a Christian may be a passive way of witnessing, but it can help sow seed, and many introverted or shy people could readily do it. I'm not suggesting that we wear a distinctive dress or exotic head covering. But, we could, for example, wear distinctive jewellery that gives us an opportunity to confess Christ in some fashion. If someone should comment on the piece, there might well be an opening for a fuller presentation of the Good News. Symbols such as a cross, a fish, a dove, a goblet, and a loaf of bread are all possibilities.

A friend of mine, Krysia, wears a lion pin because she likes it and it reminds people of Aslan in the Narnia books. This simple pin sometimes enables her to make a connection to Christ in the flow of a conversation.

I am not suggesting that we follow their tradition, but for centuries followers of Christ in the Coptic Church in Egypt have tattooed a cross on their right wrists. By doing so they have taken a bold stand in a dominant Muslim culture.

A cross might actually be the least effective symbol to wear to signify that we follow Christ, for many in the Western world wear it simply as a piece of jewellery, with no spiritual or religious significance.

I once saw Ashley, a vibrant young Christian woman, wearing around her neck a beautifully stylized emblem of an eagle. When I asked her what it signified, she referred me to Isaiah 40:31, where it is written, "But those who wait on the LORD Shall renew their strength; They shall mount up with wings like eagles" (NKJV). One can easily imagine a non-Christian friend asking her the same question and how such an inquiry might open the door to some form of witness—that she is a Christian, she waits upon God, and her strength is renewed like an eagle's.

For some Christians the idea of wearing overt or subtle Christian symbols may seem radical. But that reflects more on the Christian subculture that has taught us not to stand out or draw attention to ourselves.

The decoration of our homes is another way we can communicate some aspect of the Christian message. I know a shy and retiring woman who has a dramatic painting of Christ in her home. In the picture, Christ stands behind a bone-weary, drained man, supporting him in his fatigue and exhaustion. A closer look reveals that this sapped individual is gripping a hammer and nails in his hands. This startling painting is a mute but powerful witness to anyone who comes into that home.

This means of witness was also used in the early church. Michael Green documents that a picture found in a Christian home in the ancient ruins of Pompeii appears to have been placed in the home specifically to spark conversations with pagan visitors.[4]

Witnessing by Serving

Shy and introverted people who find it difficult to open spiritual conversations could make it a priority to serve non-Christian neighbours and friends. This may well lead to spiritual conversations. This is not only a good idea for quiet and reflective people but also obedience to the direct command of Scripture for all believers. We read in Matthew 5:16, "Let your light so shine before men, that they may see your good works and glorify your Father in heaven" (NKJV). First Peter 2:12 also calls us to the practice of carrying out good deeds for the sake of the watching world.

Tragically, in some Christian circles the teaching on the responsibility to engage in good works, which is mandated in many places throughout the New Testament, has been largely muted. Some focus so strongly on the believer always and only passively receiving from God that they never get around to teaching that God calls the Christian to a life of service and good works. It's not rocket science to conclude that kindness, goodness, and acts of service will sooner or later open a door for some kind of verbal witness.

Several years ago a tornado ripped through a neighbourhood in our city, felling many trees and causing roof damage to a few houses. Within hours a local church had workmen in the damaged area helping to bring order out of chaos. This same church has implemented Celebrate Recovery, a community-wide program that ministers to people enslaved to addictions like alcoholism, pornography, and gambling. I have been told that most of the people converted to Christ in this church in the last few years are people who have been served by this program.

Serving others can take simpler forms as well. For instance, a friend or neighbour struggling with parenting teenagers or financial problems or quitting smoking might be appreciative and open to receiving the gift of a Christian book, CD, or DVD that addresses their particular problem. Helping our neighbours shovel snow out of their driveway prepared them to accept an invitation to study the Christian faith together.

Serving doesn't take a lot of boldness or audacity. It doesn't require the shy and introverted to take the initiative in some form of aggressive witnessing. But it does show the love of God to people whom we Christians are called to love, and it does pave the way for future relationship in which a verbal witness may be shared.

If we desire to live daily taking the opportunities offered to us to witness, we must be looking for them. They are all around if we know how to watch for them. In our next section we explore the topic of how we can seize all the chances given to us.

QUESTIONS FOR GROUP DISCUSSION

1. Some people believe that only extroverted personality types are called of God to engage in witness. Do you believe that? Why or why not?

2. If, in fact, most programs that teach evangelism and witnessing are designed by extroverts, what kind of emphasis should we logically expect? What kind of an impact does this have on the introvert?

3. If you are an introvert, have you ever thought that the only way God could use you in witnessing would be by changing you into an extrovert?

4. We might view Paul as a supercharged extrovert. Are there other people in the Scriptures whom God used that we might describe as introverts?

5. What are some of the ways mentioned by which introverts can witness that are natural to their personality?

CHAPTER 10

Making the Most of Every Opportunity to Witness

> *Be wise in the way you act toward outsiders; make the most of every opportunity. Let your conversation be always full of grace, seasoned with salt, so that you may know how to answer everyone* (Colossians 4:5–6).

"Also realize that when we stand in front of God, none of us will say that we shared his Son too much. But many of us will realize that we shared his Son much too little during our time on earth." (Mark Cahill)

Sadly, far too many believers who know the Good News never or rarely share it with anyone else in spite of having many opportunities. Even those who want to witness and have had training may miss opportunities to sow seed. They might be so engrossed in their job, family, and church that they miss openings to witness. Perhaps they haven't yet adopted or even heard of the concept of seeking to daily be a witness as part of day-to-day life. That can change for the Christian who adopts the mindset, vision, and discipline to take advantage of all opportunities.

A Life of Discipleship

Witnessing and the life of discipleship must go hand in hand. Anyone can rather quickly learn the basics of how to share Christ with someone, but unless that person is walking day by day as a living, listening, active, up-to-date follower of Jesus, not much witnessing is likely to happen.

Take the importance of prayer. I put it to you that unless we are daily, hourly, weekly pursuing a walk with Christ by prayer we will have neither the boldness nor even the desire to share much about Jesus. Why do I make that claim? Because it's one thing to share the truth about a very real historical Jesus; it's quite another to share that same truth when that very morning we have been in communion by prayer with this living Christ.

The Bible in 1 Peter 3:15 calls us to "be prepared to give an answer to everyone who asks you to give the reason for the hope you have." We should think of this as not merely an intellectual readiness but a readiness that involves the spirit, emotions, and will as well. The person who follows Christ haphazardly and less than wholeheartedly will be hard pressed to share something they barely possess themselves. A disciplined, close following of Christ prepares us spiritually and mentally to "seize the day" and give fruitful witness to those who cross our path.

The famous Moravian Christians of Herrnhut of the 18th century that we discussed previously were a disciplined people who lived "on watch for the Lord," using as their motto "Our Lamb has conquered, let us follow him." They established a twenty-four hour prayer meeting, which lasted a hundred years.

They sought to be ardent disciples of Christ as they laid all at his feet and followed where he led. He rewarded them with such joy in their daily lives that they were nicknamed "God's happy people." After its first fifty years of existence, this tiny group of people had sent out some 300 missionaries to the far-flung corners of the earth.

These were a people bathed in prayer who joyfully lived lives focused on Jesus and his kingdom purposes. They will stand forever as marked examples of fervent disciples who were prepared to seize all the opportunities that came their way.

A disciplined life is one where we daily read the Scriptures and seek God in prayer. A disciplined life includes ongoing self-examination accompanied by ongoing repentance. As Socrates said, "The unexamined life is not worth living." The powerful discipline of Scripture reading and prayer should lead us to an ongoing scrutiny of our ways so that we don't live haphazardly but measure all of our deeds and the way we use time by the values that God considers important. A life of even casual discipline should lead us to committing ourselves to attending and supporting a local church, for without the strength and inspiration of others we will not do well.

SEIZING AN OPPORTUNITY

The Bible calls us to live *carpe diem,* that is, to seize the day. Now it doesn't actually use the Latin phrase, but that's what it means to "[make] the most of every opportunity" (Ephesians 5:16).

Opportunities can open up in the most unexpected ways. Once when I was in a local coffee shop I overheard some of the staff talking about the best-selling book *Fifty Shades of Grey.* I had just published a piece on the book from a Christian perspective and had also posted it on my blog. While the topic was still in the air I approached the people talking and told them that I had overheard the conversation. I identified myself as a writer who had recently published a piece on the subject. I gave them a piece of paper with my blog address written out and encouraged them to have a look at the article.

An evangelist in Columbus, South Carolina, who was a strong pro-life activist was hauled into jail for a short period of time for protesting against abortion. He immediately set up Bible studies for the prisoners and soon had more work than he could handle, witnessing to the many who gathered around him.

Paul and Silas, who were unjustly hauled into prison in the city of Philippi (Acts 16), took advantage of their situation too. Although tightly secured in stocks they sang songs and prayed to God while the other prisoners listened. Paul was not one to let any opportunity go by if he could speak a word or demonstrate by his life that he had hope and served a God who listened to prayer.

A cashier in a coffee shop once gave me back more than ten dollars extra in change. I pointed this out, and while she was fixing the error the next person waiting to be served said to me, "It's nice to see an honest man for a change."

I casually responded, "Well, I can't really take the credit; you see, I'm a Christ-follower, and he teaches me to live like that." A situation like this points out the fallacy of those who say, "I'll just live a virtuous life, and people will be drawn to Christ because of my good deeds." Although my honesty served to draw attention to myself, I had to direct the appropriate praise to Christ. If I had kept silent I would have missed an opportunity to witness to how Jesus has affected my life.

On another occasion, while on our way to a birthday party my wife and I prayed for an opportunity to bless people with a word of witness. But truth be told, I don't think either of us had much faith that it was going to happen in a party context. We arrived early and were introduced to a young woman I'll call Doris, with whom we shared a lively, friendly conversation. While I was chatting with friends later in the evening, Doris left the dance floor, came over, and invited me to dance with her. Normally I would have been happy to accept. But I was sitting next to a couple of fundamentalist Christians, and I was concerned that I would offend them by accepting. So even though she kept on asking, I kept on refusing.

Finally she said, in evident hurt and disbelief, "So you really are turning me down."

Deeply concerned now about offending her, I stood up and said to her, "Doris, you have greatly honoured me by your invitation, and I would love to, but please believe me that I simply cannot."

At that she sat down beside me, and we proceeded to talk. She wanted to know about my church, my faith, where I was preaching and more. In the ten minutes that followed, even though we were next to the dance floor and in the midst of a hubbub of conversations, it was like the world stopped and the only people in it were Doris and I, alone. I saw that this was God's answer to the earlier prayer. So I quickly laid out for my new friend my core belief in Jesus Christ and his mission of coming to call sinners to repentance and faith.

As Doris listened I could see deep interest and a kind of wistfulness on her face. It turned out that she had had some kind of Christian influence on her life when she was just a girl. The conversation soon turned to other themes, and the "magical" moment passed. Or so it seemed.

Then just before she stood up to leave, Doris expressed her thanks. We were sitting closely together, and she leaned forward in her chair and gently and tenderly kissed me, first on my right cheek and then on my left. It was a most chaste, solemn, and profound kind of thanks. It left me quite moved and full of joy at her response upon hearing the truth about Jesus.

Using Unexpected Situations

On different occasions people may approach us proselytizing, selling their wares, conducting a survey, or for any number of purposes. At times we can use these opportunities for witness.

Once a young woman came to our door selling books on health issues put out by a religious sect, which I identified by looking at the publisher. After we had talked about the books and made other small talk I asked if I could ask her a couple of questions. She agreed, and I asked her two significant questions: "If you were to die tonight, do you have a complete assurance that you would go to heaven? If you were to die tonight and stand before God and he were to say to you, 'Why should I let you into my heaven?' What would you say to him?" On the basis of her answers and because she was open I gave her a full presentation of the gospel and challenged her to make sure of her salvation.

Once when I was in a shopping mall a young person asked if I was willing to do a quick shopping survey. I agreed to do so, but when the survey was over I asked if I might do a quick survey of my own. She agreed, and I asked the two questions just mentioned. Although she belonged to a well-known evangelical church, she had no assurance and almost no understanding of the Good News. I was late for an appointment, so all I could do was to tell her that she was lacking something of great importance and strongly encourage her to talk to her pastor.

As this story demonstrates, we should never take it for granted that the person sitting in the pew beside us truly knows, understands, and has responded to the gospel. We who faithfully go to church should be careful to talk about the Good News of Christ among ourselves. Not only will it build us up in our most holy faith, but it also will be a form of witness and evangelism to those who are not truly converted.

On one occasion I met a man at a conference who had been raised in a staid, solid mainline church, with a reputation for knowing and preaching the gospel and being careful about teaching accurate doctrine. Nevertheless this man shared that, although he had gone through the church rituals and had ended up in positions of leadership, one day through the witness of another person he realized that he was "in the church" but not "in Christ." He shared with excitement how he had personally put his faith and trust in Christ that day and had been born again.

Justin Martyr, one of the early Church Fathers, was exploring various philosophies in his pursuit of truth before his conversion around AD 130. Shortly before he surrendered to the claims of Christ he came into contact with a Christian who was a complete stranger to him. *Christian History* magazine reports the story as follows:

> It occurred during his years of spiritual searching, when he was reading philosopher after philosopher to understand the meaning of life. One day while strolling on a beach in Ephesus, Justin met an old man, who engaged him in a discussion about philosophy. It was but one conversation, and Justin never saw the man again. But this one conversation kindled in him, he said, a love for the prophets and for "friends of Christ." Not long after that conversation, Justin converted.[1]

> The old man on the beach that day met a seeker, and he, doubtless led by the Spirit, seized the opportunity

to witness to this total stranger. That stranger would one day become an apologist and later be renowned as one of the early Church Fathers. History has not recorded the identity of the old man Justin Martyr met, but God certainly knows his identity and has undoubtedly marked his faithfulness.

Some time ago while I was walking to find my car in a large parking lot on a dark and foggy night I made an interesting observation. While yet a little distance from the parking lot I could see the many, many lights that lit up the acres of cars. From a distance, because the fog clearly outlined just how far the light travelled, I could see that each one of these lights was providing a cone of light in the darkness. No, there weren't enough lights to illuminate the whole parking lot, but where the lights were they were clearly driving back the darkness under them.

In the same way we who believe in Christ can and do provide light in the areas of darkness that we inhabit. We do not have to take on the task of lighting the whole world—a job far too big for us mere mortals—but we are called to, and indeed we can, light up the area that we are in. And there is no better way for us to fulfill our mission than by courageously, consistently, carefully shining the light of the Good News of Jesus to all who live in that darkness.

QUESTIONS FOR GROUP DISCUSSION

1. How are discipleship and witnessing related to one another? Does a fresh, up-to-date experience with Jesus affect the quality of our witness?

2. Read Acts 16 and then discuss how Paul and Silas seized a painful opportunity to engage in witnessing. On the surface does it seem like a good opportunity? Why or why not?

3. From time to time unexpected opportunities for witnessing will come our way. What is the secret to grabbing those moments and making them fruitful moments of witness?

The Lost Doctrine of Repentance

In 2010 I attended a major men's conference, where thousands and thousands of men, many of them not believers, had come to hear messages by motivational speakers and preachers. Although I listened intently I was unable to discern any focus on the need to turn from sin as one was turning to Jesus. It simply was not there. As well, believing or trusting in Jesus was weakly presented, and there was little mention of Christ's substitutionary atonement.

If this had been a conference set up by the so-called liberal churches who long ago abandoned the Bible and have largely abandoned belief in a historical Jesus, it would be one thing—but this conference was set up, promoted by, and executed by a national evangelical organization.

Sadly, a focus on repentance is also missing in many evangelical churches. A good many pastors, I fear, often present the Good News of Christ without mentioning one word about the need to turn from sin. As a result, people are given the good news that one can receive eternal life by believing in Christ, but they hear nothing about turning away from sin.

"To repent" fundamentally means "to change one's mind," and it is almost invariably used in Scripture to express the changing of one's mind or attitude toward sin. Since repentance means to change one's mind and to turn away from sin, it directly implies that the person involved is acknowledging the lordship of Christ over his or her life. In large part then, the willingness to repent means that the seeker is acknowledging that God is sovereign, that he has the total right of command over all of his or her life.

CULTURAL OPPOSITION

Why are some otherwise doctrinally sound churches missing the boat on this crucial element of gospel teaching?

A key element links directly to the culture and the times in which we live. Sin and vice have become so common, so accepted, and so normalized that many people are apt to take offense when they are called to turn from sin. The government itself is encouraging people to believe that it is their right to never be offended about anything. Indeed, human rights tribunals and commissions have been set up in Canada to help punish people who have offended their fellow citizens.

An example of this new reality has to do with the institution of marriage. In the past when a minister preached on a biblical passage indicating that God from the beginning established marriage as a one woman–one man relationship, there was little danger of offending anyone. However, defending traditional marriage today is seen as an attack on a group of people; it is seen as bigotry. A good many people believe that defending opposite-sex marriage is immoral, for the new, largely accepted, secular morality believes that gay marriage is good, the new norm, and perfectly acceptable. The result is that some pastors who do not want to be called bigots or perceived as controversial will no longer clearly teach that traditional marriage is the biblical norm. They are tempted to be silent about the elephant in the room—gay marriage—and will studiously avoid challenging the new norms that promote it. To be sure, these pastors have not changed their views; they have simply come to the conclusion that it is safer to avoid the subject.

Some pastors avoid such topics because they want to be sensitive to the culture and sensitive to individuals who have been "hurt" by the church. They do not see that in their sensitivity to the culture they neglect to teach the full truth of God's word and so end up giving partial truth to the flock under their care. Tragically, this is an example of hurting the many, including the coming generations, so that a few may be spared the pain of hearing plainly spoken truth.

The very sad end result for people in the pews is that they will be forced to reach their own theological conclusions from information gleaned from newspapers and other mass media. Does anyone believe they will hear God's word through the lens of the mass media? They will in fact imbibe a worldview of marriage that is hostile to biblical Christianity.

In addition to receiving pressure from outside the church, church leaders are also influenced by pressure from some within the church who greatly minimize preaching on repentance.

Those doing this would deny that it is their intent, but ultimately it is the effect of their teaching. David Kinnaman, president of Barna Group, and his co-author Gabe Lyons make the case in their book *Unchristian* that Christians have an image problem because "We have become famous for what we oppose, rather than who we are for."[1] He concludes that believers get a bad rap because they take strong stands on certain issues. The authors consider these strong stands to be counterproductive because Christians, ironically, are perceived as *unchristian* in seeking to hold to biblical standards. Kinnaman and Lyons claim that coming to Jesus is a very simple thing and emphasize that there are no "hoops to jump through."[2] They cite Acts 2:37–41 to buttress their claim. Unfortunately for them, the text in question specifically calls for repentance and baptism to be applied to those who want to come to Christ.

This is an example of a dangerous minimizing of "turning from sin," a crucial point of theology that the church forgets at its own peril. I believe there is no true conversion, and therefore no subsequent transformation, in anybody's life apart from repentance.

I am not unsympathetic to the view that Christians often have an image problem. I furthermore believe some of that problem is associated with judgmentalism and a speaking of truth in less than a loving manner. However, the major problem of our day is that to a hyper-tolerant, sin-loving culture Christians often appear to be unloving simply because we are faithful to Scripture. Kinnaman sees this as a problem and would like Christians to tone down their rhetoric on what is moral and not moral to make the church more inviting and friendly to those on the outside looking in. If Kinnaman is trying to get the church to speak in a more loving tone, that's certainly a good thing. But I get the impression from his book that he wants believers to very much tone down their moral certainty so that we will not offend people who possess no such certainty.

I have expressed earlier in this book that part of our duty of love is to present the whole gospel, which includes the "bad" news that there is sin and we are sinners and then the good news of a Saviour who forgives real sin and sinners. The early church did this in the time of the Roman Empire (see appendix 2 on how early Christians faced persecution). It is interesting that they too by Kinnaman's definition had an image problem—they were known at times as "haters of mankind." I strongly believe that true Christianity will always have an "image" problem, will always have a public relations problem. That is part of the cross we are called to carry. It is not a cross we have permission to put down.

NEGATIVE EFFECT

Another reason for the neglect of repentance may be that pastors and preachers see this teaching as a negative thing. I think most of us would agree that people in general don't want to hear a negative message about their sins and shortcomings. So for leaders to place appropriate emphasis on the negative and risk offending people takes ongoing courage to simply stand against the tide.

Some Christians actually have a theological motivation for neglecting the doctrine of repentance. The so-called "positive confession" evangelicals, for example, with their trademark emphasis on confessing only positive things at all times, have almost certainly left their mark, to the detriment of solid biblical preaching. Indeed, I once heard a pastor of this persuasion preaching in a most apologetic manner for saying some negative things. Given his theological stance he felt he was treading on shaky ground. How very sad! The Bible from cover to cover is full of the "negative message" that men and women have fallen into sin and need to be rescued by believing the proclamation of the Good News of Jesus Christ. But not until they understand the bad news of our human condition will they be open to the good news of redemption through Jesus.

Francis Schaeffer, a prominent theologian of the 1970s, once said that if he only had an hour to spend with an unbeliever he would spend forty-five of those minutes seeking to show the person the problem, and then would devote the other fifteen minutes to sharing Christ as the solution.[3]

Questions for Group Discussion

1. How is the call to repentance (perceived by some to be negative) actually a key part of the Good News that we share?

2. Just how prominent a place did Jesus and the apostles give the preaching of repentance?

3. If repentance fundamentally means to turn away from one's sins, is it likely that it is a teaching that will offend at least some people?

4. In a society awash with the idea that no one has the right to offend anyone else, is it conceivable that repentance might be played down in many churches for fear of offending people?

5. Are at least some in the church in danger of losing this key doctrine of repentance because of the tendency to put good public relations ahead of solid doctrine and teaching?

Persecution of the Early Christians in the Roman Empire

> "We are but of yesterday, but we have filled every
> place among you—cities, islands, fortresses, towns,
> market places, the very camp, tribes, companies,
> palace, senate, forum—we have left nothing to you
> but the temples of your gods." (Tertullian)

Shortly before Jesus went to his death on the cross he had a deeply personal meeting with his disciples around the Passover meal. In that special time of communion known as the upper room discourse, Jesus shared a sobering truth with his disciples. He warned them in John 15:19 that they would be hated by the world. He went on to tell them that he would be persecuted, and they should expect the same kind of treatment (v. 20). Jesus was laying out the truth that persecution from the world should not be regarded as abnormal for his followers but rather to be expected and anticipated as part of the life of following Christ. Paul the apostle confirmed the same truth when he wrote in 2 Timothy 3:12, "In fact, everyone who wants to live a godly life in Christ Jesus will be persecuted."

It appears from the book of Acts that the early church had a brief honeymoon period after the day of Pentecost in which they were free from persecution. But when Peter and John healed the cripple at the temple door in Acts 3, which resulted in more preaching and many more conversions, the honeymoon period ended. The Jewish leaders came after the apostles, hauling them before their courts and issuing dire threats that they must stop preaching and teaching in Jesus' name. This they refused to do, and their perseverance was rewarded with seeing many miracles and many, many people coming into the kingdom, including a number of priests (Acts 6:7).

In Acts 6 Stephen is described as a man filled with "God's grace and power" because he performed many miraculous signs and wonders. Beyond that he also spoke powerfully, for his accusers could not stand up "against his wisdom or the Spirit by whom he spoke" (Acts 6:10).

God was using the ministry of Stephen in a remarkable way, but this in turn drew the attention of the authorities, who called false witnesses to testify against him before the Jewish law courts. Remarkably, even in the face of this attack Stephen was undeterred. Taking the opportunity given to him he preached a sermon of witness to the whole accusing body and concluded by flinging into their teeth the charge that they were a stiff-necked people, always resisting the Holy Spirit, and that they had betrayed and murdered the Righteous One (Acts 7:51–52).

Stephen was stoned to death for his faithful proclamation. But it should capture our attention that even in the face of persecution he refused to keep quiet about the truth and spoke it in white hot fashion. He obviously considered the speaking of the truth more important than the safety of his own person. He knew his persecutors were capable of killing him. But that did not hold him back from speaking boldly.

The Bible records in Acts the travels and indefatigable ministry of the apostle Paul. Immediately after his stunning conversion on the road to Damascus he began to preach in the synagogues of Damascus that Jesus was the Son of God (Acts 9:20). The Jews in that city hatched a plot to kill him. However, Paul learned of their plot and escaped to Jerusalem after his brothers in the faith lowered him from a basket through an opening in the city wall (Acts 9:25).

Much of the rest of the book of Acts is devoted to Paul's missionary journeys. Those who regularly read the Bible get used to the stories of Paul's many persecutions and tend to take them for granted. But if we step back for a moment and analyze what was happening to him on a regular basis, it is quite astonishing. He travelled frequently on his missionary journeys, and the pattern is boringly predicable. He arrived in a new city and began to witness and preach that Jesus was the Christ and people needed to turn to him. Sooner or later—usually sooner—he caught the attention of the Jewish leaders, who stirred up trouble against him and began to persecute him. Riots broke out, conspiracies to kill him were hatched, he got hauled before authorities, he got the lash, he was placed in prison, and on occasion he was stoned. None of this however seemed to slow him down.

One gets the impression that Paul took the attitude that persecution was part of the price of doing the business of preaching the gospel. It didn't seem to deter him, depress him, or discourage him in any way. He would rise from the pile of stones hurled with killing intent, dust himself off, and go on to the next city to continue preaching the Christ he loved (Acts 14:19–20).

The new movement that came to be known as Christianity was born while the Roman Empire was still flourishing. Indeed, the empire endured for almost five more centuries, until the last emperor, Romulus Augustus, was deposed in AD 476 by the barbarian Odoacer.

By the first century Rome had implicitly granted to Judaism an established religious status as a *religio licita*. Historians disagree whether such status was officially promulgated or was simply a matter of local officials reacting to local circumstances. In any case, Christianity at the beginning did not possess such a status, and for a good deal of its early history its converts were persecuted and harassed by both the Jews and the wider Roman society. Roman authorities were not at all reluctant to add other gods to their pantheon of deities, which they did as a matter of policy when they conquered new countries with new gods.[1] Why, then, were Christians not given the same status that Judaism and other religions enjoyed?

There were a number of contributing factors, but mainly it was because Christianity was not identified with a particular nation-state as were the other religions that had accepted status. Also, in its early days Christianity was viewed with hostility because the authorities saw it as a dangerous superstition practiced mostly by the lower classes. Thus it was held in contempt and depreciated. Only later on when Constantine and Licinius passed the Edict of Milan in AD 313 did it begin to attain the standing that other religions had enjoyed for centuries.

For Rome the state cult of emperor worship performed an important unifying function by elevating the emperors to the status of gods. Citizens were freely allowed to worship whatever permitted god they wanted to as long as they also agreed to participate in emperor worship. However, Christians not only worshipped in a non-permitted religion, but they also refused to have anything to do with emperor worship. Since these early believers knew there was only one Lord—the Lord Jesus Christ, to whom they gave their full worship—they simply would not burn incense before a statue of the emperor and say the words "Caesar is Lord." Although it was not enforced equally throughout the empire, Christians were at times caught between their loyalty to Christ and the deference they were required to pay to the state. Their refusal to bow before the Roman gods was treated as criminal obstinacy and as adequate justification for the death penalty.[2]

Strange though it may sound, these early Christians were accused of being atheists. As Carl Henry puts it, "For ancient Roman thought the spiritual enemy was atheism, and Christianity was reckoned to be exactly that."[3] In part the charge of atheism stuck because the Christian God was invisible, and of course the believers refused to build idols. They were also seen as atheists because they refused to acknowledge any of the divinities of the Roman pantheon. They acknowledged only one God and his Son, Jesus Christ.

This exclusive loyalty was seen as an offense against the concept of divinity itself. And since god and state were so intertwined, Christians, logically, were viewed as disloyal to the state and akin to traitors. This is why their punishment was so harsh. Furthermore, they were viewed as dangerously impious people by their fellow Romans. And this impiety made people furious, for many Romans believed that the gods were likely to become angry at such disrespect and bring calamity of various kinds upon the whole empire.

The Christians, because of slander against them and their own penchant for secrecy, soon came to have a very low social image among their contemporaries. They were actually accused of practicing incest and being cannibals. These were very serious charges, and one wonders how such accusations ever saw the light of day. According to Michael Green it had to do in part with their practice of meeting secretly in special meetings where only believers were present. In addition to that, "they used realistic language about feeding on Christ in the Eucharist, and they spoke of loving fellow-Christians, whom they called brothers and sisters in Christ. Gossiping lips and dirty minds did all the rest."[4] Regardless of how the accusations came about, the very fact that they did shows that at least some in Roman society had a deep contempt for the people known as Christians.

Christians apparently took seriously (some have suggested too seriously) the scriptural command found in 2 Corinthians 6:17: "Therefore come out from them and be separate, says the Lord. Touch no unclean thing, and I will receive you." The believers separated themselves so thoroughly from the various Roman institutions that the citizens of the empire came near to seeing them as belonging to something other than the human race.[5]

Life in Roman culture was lived in the midst of casual idolatries and immoralities that were practiced every day. Green notes,

> Thus the Christian would not attend gladiatorial shows or games or plays. He would not read pagan literature. He would not enlist as a soldier…He would not be painter or sculptor, for that would be to acquiesce in idolatry. Nor would he be a schoolmaster, for then he would inevitably have to tell the immoral stories of the pagan gods. The Christian had better steer clear of

business contracts, because these required the taking of oaths which the Christian abjured.[6]

And on and on it went. The believers desiring to live a holy life cut themselves off from so much of daily cultural activity that they were regarded as "haters of the human race."

They were regarded as social misfits because they actively shunned Roman society and tried to live on its fringes as far away from the contamination of idolatry as they could. The Romans, believing that they themselves represented the epitome of advanced culture and manners, were galled to no end. It seemed to them that a bunch of upstart, ragamuffin, ostensibly morally derelict people from the lower classes was standing in judgment on their institutions and way of life.

Because they were viewed as haters of mankind, misfits, and impious atheists, believers were persecuted at various times in a variety of ways. However it is a mistake to assume that the persecution in the first three hundred years was uniformly applied throughout the empire. Furthermore there were relatively long periods of time when persecutions were comparatively mild.

There were times however when even self-identifying as a Christian was dangerous for a Roman believer. Pliny the Younger, a Roman official, on a visit to northern Turkey encountered Christians and had reason to question them. He urged them to recant, giving them three opportunities; if the individual refused to comply, he was deemed worthy of punishment.[7] In this case it appears that Christians were not being mistreated for supposed crimes but rather for the "crime" of being followers of Christ.

But most of the time there were specific charges and accusations that were leveled at these Christians, who were considered beneath contempt. Conspiracy, illegal association, and enmity toward the gods of Rome were the charges formed against Christians so that they could be punished in various forms.[8] Another very common charge repeatedly hurled at Christians was the indictment of being obstinately superstitious. Now what did they mean by the term "superstition"? According to a number of prominent Romans, including Cicero and Plutarch, the charge referred to "any offensive religious belief or practice that deviated from Roman norms."[9]

Nero unleashed an attack against the Christians in AD 64 by accusing them of being the arsonists who had caused the great fire that year. Some historians believe that Nero himself ordered the fire to be set so that he could fulfill his dream of a grand rebuilding of the city. If true, Nero found the perfect scapegoat to cover his crime. Not many in the population would have cared to defend this hated minority when Nero seized many believers and put them to death in fiendishly imaginative ways. Tacitus, reporting on this incident, described the Christians as "a class hated for their abominations" and guilty of "hatred of the human race."[10]

In AD 253–260, Emperor Valerian unleashed an attack of significant magnitude. Many bishops, priests, and deacons were executed, and church property was confiscated. Christians who had been imperial civil servants were consigned to slavery, and believers were forbidden to worship in their cemeteries, which previously had been considered sacrosanct.[11] In AD 304 Galerius, a military commander and direct assistant to Emperor Diocletian, worked on measures to strengthen the cult of emperor worship. He therefore mandated that Christians throughout the empire had to make sacrifices, on pain of death if they refused.[12]

Believers living in the last half of the Roman Empire had to steel themselves against any number of severe penalties that a persecuting state was wont to inflict. Over the years they were tortured, crucified, burned at the stake, beheaded, thrown to wild animals, and exiled to desolate islands or to the salt mines. At times their Scriptures were confiscated, their property was appropriated, they were forbidden the right of assembly with one another, they were forbidden to carry out worship, and buildings for worship were destroyed.

When the church was born it was definitely not an easy time to be a Christian. Followers of Judaism, the seedbed of the church, were hostile from the start and grew increasingly hostile as the faith took hold. In short order the gospel was offered to the Gentiles as well as the Jews. But the Roman world of the time had a well-defined worldview of its own. And Romans were not at all inclined to immediately bow to Christ upon hearing of him. Indeed, it took about 250 years of unrelenting work and witness with intermittent persecution before the church came to a place of sufficient power to be formally tolerated in the Roman world.

It should grab our attention that a tiny despised minority of Christ-followers, by the model of their upright lives, their willingness to speak the truth of the gospel, and their courage to suffer persecution, hugely impacted the hostile world in which they lived. In time Christians could be found in every strata of Roman society, from the lowliest slave quarters to households of the rich and powerful, including the emperor himself.

There is little doubt that it would have been far safer to worship in one of the many pagan temples in Rome than to be a follower of Christ. If ever there was a time for keeping your mouth shut and your head down, surely that was it. Yet the picture that comes down to us from the historical record portrays Christians as ones who refused to be silent. They testified to the Christ who had saved them, and they did not shrink back from announcing that he was coming back to judge the world. Believers did not hide their light under a basket, but they looked for ways to spread the truth among neighbours, friends, fellow slaves, and people they worked with. Neither outright persecution nor its threat was able to stop Christ-followers from witnessing to the gospel. And God faithfully used the light of this puny, despised little band of people to bring millions of Romans to Christ so that by AD 300 there were approximately 6,300,000 Christians scattered throughout the Roman Empire.[13]

Resources for Sharing the Good News

Christianity Explored: An excellent DVD series. The website and locations to order material may be accessed at www. ceministries.org.

Evangelism Explosion: An older but still useful tool for sharing the Good News. The website may be accessed at http://www.eecanada.org/home.html.

Just Walk Across the Room: The Just Walk experience originated from a series of five talks delivered during midweek services by Bill Hybels, the founding senior pastor of Willow Creek Community Church. The result was *Just Walk Across the Room: The Four-Week Church Campaign,* an experience intended to put a blowtorch to the value of personal evangelism in your church. The curriculum may be ordered from www.amazon. com.

Acts 29 Sharing Course: Material can be ordered from www.navpress.com or phone 1–800–366–7788.

Irresistible Evangelism: This is a website that is well worth looking at. It can be accessed at www.godsgps.com.

Xenos Christian Fellowship: A very valuable website, which includes downloadable resources on evangelism: www.xenos.org.

H2O Evangelistic DVD series: https://www.visionvideo.com/search_by_text.taf?_function=text_list&keyword=h20.

Some Useful Books

How to Give Away Your Faith by Paul Little
Lifestyle Evangelism by Joe Aldrich
Stop Witnessing and Start Loving by Paul Borthwick
The Art of Personal Evangelism by Will McRaney Jr.
Out of the Saltshaker and Into the World: Evangelism as a Way of Life by Rebecca Pippert
Evangelism in the Early Church by Michael Green
Introverts in the Church by Adam S. McHugh
Questioning Evangelism by Randy Newman
Evangelism Is…How to Share Jesus with Passion and Confidence by D. Early and D. Wheeler
Evangelism without Additives by Jim Henderson

Endnotes

Chapter 1—Called To Witness

1. Richard Bond, "Understanding a Relational Model of Evangelism and How It Relates to Evangelism Explosion," youthee.net/articles/relmodelee.htm, accessed August 28, 2012.

2. Chris A. Castaldo, *Holy Ground: Walking with Jesus as a Former Catholic* (Grand Rapids, Michigan: Zondervan, 2009), 171.

3. Ileana Llorens, "John 3:16: Meaning Of Tim Tebow's Touted Bible Verse And A Look Into Religion In Sports," *The Huffington Post,*
http://www.huffingtonpost.com/2012/01/10/john-316-tim-tebow-bible_n_1195221.html.

4. Ibid.

Chapter 2—Liberating Ourselves From False Concepts, Part I

Lillian Kwon, "Calif. Evangelist: We're Just No Good at Evangelism," CP Church and Ministries, http://www.christianpost.com/news/evangelist-were-just-no-good-at-evangelism-45800/.

2. Don Feder, "Why Hollywood Hates Christianity," FrontPageMagazine.com, archive.frontpagemag.com/readArticle.aspx?ARTID=12835.

3. Margaret Atwood, *Bluebeard's Egg* (Toronto: McClelland and Stewart, 1984), 169.

4. Brit Hume, *Tiger Woods Should Turn to the Christian Faith to Find Forgiveness and Redemption,* http://www.youtube.com/watch?v=XZ9Ek30Kk9Q.

Chapter 3—Liberating Ourselves From False Concepts, Part II

1. Michael Patton, "Should Christians Have Unbelieving Friends?" bible.org, http://bible.org/article/should-christians-have-unbelieving-friends.

2. R. Larry Moyer, *Twenty-One Things God Never Said* (Grand Rapids, Michigan: Kregel Publications, 2004), 33.

3. Ibid., 30.

Chapter 4—The Power Source

1. Neil Cole, *Search & Rescue: Becoming a Disciple Who Makes a Difference* (Grand Rapids, Michigan: Baker Books, 2008), 187.

2. Leslie K. Tarr, "A Prayer Meeting that Lasted 100 Years," *Christian History,* no. 1 (1982): 18.

3. Ibid., 18.

4. Matthew Henry, *Matthew Henry's Commentary* (Old Tappan, New Jersey: Fleming H. Revell Company, 1708), 1219.

5. F. F. Bruce, *Commentary on the Book of Acts* (Grand Rapids, Michigan: Wm. B. Eerdmans, 1974), 99.

6. W. Carey Moore, ed., "Baptized Into One Spirit," *Christian History,* no. 1 (1982): 25.

Chapter 5—The Content of Our Witness

1. Ray Comfort, *God Has A Wonderful Plan for Your Life: The Myth of the Modern Message* (Bellflower, CA: Living Waters Publications, 2010), 69–71.

Chapter 7—Building Bridges

"Potty-Mouthed Canadians," City News, http://www.citynews.ca/2010/08/05/potty-mouthed-canadians/.

2. William L. Turner, *Anywhere, Anytime* (Valley Forge, Pennsylvania: Judson Press, 1997), 17.

Chapter 9—How Can the Introverted Carry Out Their Witness?

1. Adam S. McHugh, *Introverts in the Church: Finding Our Place in an Extroverted Culture* (Downers Grove, Illinois: Intervarsity Press, 2009), 35–38.

2. Ibid., 42.

3. Ibid., 172.

4. Michael Green, *Evangelism in the Early Church* (Grand Rapids, Michigan: William B. Eerdmans), 216.

Chapter 10—Making The Most of Every Opportunity to Witness

1. E. Glenn Hinson, "Ordinary Saints at First Church," *Christian History*, no. 57 (1998): 20.

Appendix 1—The Lost Doctrine of Repentance

1. David Kinnaman and Gabe Lyons, *Unchristian: What a New Generation Really Thinks About Christianity….and Why It Matters* (Grand Rapids, Michigan: Baker Books, 2007), 26.

2. Ibid., 79.

3. Jim Elliff, "So What's the Problem?" Christian Communicators Worldwide, 2001, http://www.ccwtoday.org/article_view.asp?article_id=165.

Appendix 2—Persecution of the Early Christians in the Roman Empire

1. Green, *Evangelism,* 35.

2. Ibid., 43.

3. Carl F. H. Henry, *Twilight of a Great Civilization: The Drift Toward Neo-Paganism* (Westchester, Illinois: Crossway Books, 1988), 179.

4. Green, *Evangelism,* 39.

5. Ibid., 40–41.

6. Ibid., 40.

7. J. David Cassel, "Defending the Cannibals," *Christian History*, no. 57 (1998): 13.

8. Everett Ferguson, "Persecution in the Early Church: Did You Know?" *Christian History*, no. 27 (1990): 9.

9. Cassel, "Defending the Cannibals," 13.

10. "Nero's Cruelties," *Christian History*, no. 27 (1990): 6.

11. Ibid., 10.

12. Ibid., 10.

13. Rodney Stark, *The Rise of Christianity: How the Obscure, Marginal Jesus Movement Became the Dominant Religious Force in the Western World in a Few Centuries* (Princeton, New Jersey: Princeton University Press, 1996), 7.

About the Author

R oyal Hamel is an ordained minister with the Christian and Missionary Alliance. He served with the Alliance, as a pastor and cross-cultural worker, for twenty-two years. He has pastored churches in Mica Creek, British Columbia; Regina, Saskatchewan; Buenos Aires, Argentina; and Guelph, Ontario. He holds credentials in the Central Canadian District of the Christian and Missionary Alliance. He and his family are part of the Crossings Alliance Church in Acton, Ontario.

Royal completed studies at Canadian Bible College in the early '70s, spent a year in the missions program at Canadian Theological Seminary and completed his formal training when he graduated with a Master of Theological Studies from Gordon-Conwell Theological Seminary in 1980. Royal and his wife, Linda, have three sons and live in Guelph, Ontario.

He is the founder and director of Light the Darkness Ministries, a non-profit organization whose mission is to teach and inspire new ways of taking the Good News of Christ into the culture. LDM offers Talk the Walk seminars for the purpose of inspiring and training believers to more effectively and boldly share their faith. LDM is also concerned with boldly upholding biblical truth in an age that seems to be running the other way.

For more information about Light the Darkness Ministries
and its programs visit
www.lightthedarkness.org
or contact Royal directly at
www.royalhamel.com.

Muzzle Removal 101

1. Undo muzzle straps by gathering 2-5 friends to study book together.
2. Pray daily for the power of the Holy Spirit (Acts 1:8).
3. Discard dangling muzzle—begin with baby steps to bleat your witness, praying always.
4. Stomp on muzzle, honor Christ and obey him daily with your new lifestyle of sharing.

To book a speaking engagement with Royal please visit www.royalhamel.com.